A TALE OF
TWO KINGDOMS

JOHN RING

A TALE OF
TWO KINGDOMS

Living Your Citizenship In God's Kingdom

PARADIGM
PUBLISHING

Copyright © 2007 Paradigm Publishing
1965 Lakepointe Drive,
Lewisville, Texas, 75057, U.S.A.
All rights reserved.

Unless otherwise indicated, all scripture quotations
are from the New American Standard Bible® Update - 1995

Scripture taken from the NEW AMERICAN STANDARD Bible®
Copyright © 1960, 1962, 1963, 1968, 1971, 1972, 1973, 1975, 1977, 1995
by The Lockman Foundation.
Used by permission.

Scripture taken from the Amplified® Bible
Copyright © 1954, 1958, 1962, 1964, 1965, 1987
by The Lockman Foundation.
Used by permission.

Scripture taken from the New King James Version.
Copyright © 1982 by Thomas Nelson, Inc.
Used by permission.
All rights reserved.

Scripture quotations marked NLT are taken from
the Holy Bible, New Living Translation, copyright 1996, 2004.
Used by permission of Tyndale House Publishers, Inc.,
Wheaton, Illinois 60189. All rights reserved.

Scripture taken from the HOLY BIBLE, NEW INTERNATIONAL VERSION®.
Copyright © 1973, 1978, 1984 International Bible Society.
Used by permission of Zondervan.
All rights reserved.

ISBN 1-934143-99-5

Printed in the United States of America

Without limiting the rights under copyright reserved above, no part of this publication may be reproduced, stored in or introduced into a retrieval system, or transmitted, in any form or by any means (electronic, mechanical, photocopying, recording, or otherwise), without the prior written permission of both the copyright owner and the above publisher of this book.
Your support of the author's rights is appreciated.

ACKNOWLEDGMENTS

Many things were involved in bringing this book to print. Two men have had enormous impact on me and I would like to dedicate this work to them. Rob Wheeler planted a seed of the kingdom in my heart thirty years ago, and Dick Benjamin, the apostle from Abbott Loop Community Church, prepared a field for that seed to grow. I am grateful to both men for their commitment to the Lord, their citizenship in the kingdom, and their influence on this work and my life.

I would like to give many thanks to everyone at Paradigm Publishing, whose blood, sweat, and tears brought this book to print. Special thanks to Amy Nash for her work managing the project. Also, thanks to Virginia Thomas and Lauren Hartley, who lost much sleep in order to finish the technical edit in an amazingly short time. Thanks also to Elizabeth Froeberg and Michelle Petty for their editing contributions and Rashaell Amarillas for her hard work in pre-submission proofing.

Three people prepared the road that led to this book's publication. I am grateful to Johnny Combs, whose passion for the kingdom caused him to support the book's completion and whose belief in the project opened the door for it to come to print. I also would like to thank my son Shawn, whose walk with God and belief in the message caused him to support the project going forward. Lastly and most importantly, special thanks to my wife whose prayers, intercession, and commitment to me, kept me moving forward with the Lord.

Most of all of course, I am grateful to the King of Kings and Lord of Lords, who saw fit to pull me from the kingdom of darkness and give me citizenship in His kingdom, and who is willing to use flawed vessels to do His work. Thank you, Jesus.

Contents

Prologue	1
Chapter 1 - The Fall and Rule of Satan	7
Chapter 2 - The Lie	13
Chapter 3 - The Announcement	25
Chapter 4 - The Defeat of the Prince of Darkness	39
Chapter 5 - The Naturalization Process	55
Chapter 6 - Entering The Kingdom of Light	69
Chapter 7 - Your Mission, Should You Choose To Accept It	81
Intermission	97
Chapter 8 - Walking In All Your Citizenship Provides	103
Chapter 9 - Finding "Rest" In The Kingdom	117
Chapter 10 - Kingdom Economics 101	133
Chapter 11 - What The Kingdom of God Is Like	153
Chapter 12 - Maintaining Your Supply Lines	169
Epilogue	187

Prologue

"It was the best of times, it was the worst of times, it was the age of wisdom, it was the age of foolishness, it was the epoch of belief, it was the epoch of incredulity, it was the season of Light, it was the season of Darkness ..."
Charles Dickens—A Tale of Two Cities

Charles Dickens explored two radically different cultures existing in the same time at the same place. In our world today, two cultures even more dramatically opposed are battling to the death. The cultures—these kingdoms—are of much greater eternal impact than Dickens' revolutionaries, and yet too many of us know the Dickens classic better than the kingdoms fighting for our attention.

There is a kingdom on earth today whose citizens walk in freedom, joy, and delight—whose God is more able than one can imagine. Defeat is not their portion. Fear is not their portion. Discouragement is not their portion. Victory belongs to them! They are "more than conquerors" the Bible says. They are mighty men and women of great boldness.

Is this your experiential walk in Christ? It wasn't mine. Do you have "more than conquerors" as your testimony or do you limp along in abject survival, thanking God you haven't been destroyed? I can not begin to tell you how long I simply survived! The knowledge of the kingdoms helped me receive the revelation of the kingdom, but the revelation is setting me free. Revelation is ongoing—continuous, not static—so it will unfold gradually over time. Everything is built on what goes before, so gaining the insight and knowledge is beneficial. However, it is not the reality. Living it is the reality. Walking in faith with knowledge is the reality. Having the power of God in your life is the reality. My hope is that this book will cause you to long for God's kingdom until you begin to find it. My prayer for you is that you will become aware of its existence in a much greater way, so you will begin to hunt for it, pursue it, and won't be dissuaded from finding it until its revelation is complete in you.

The two eternal kingdoms are referred to by many opposing titles: the kingdom of darkness and the kingdom of light; the kingdom of this world and the kingdom of heaven. Each is controlled by different rules of conduct and governed by a different set of laws and principles. The two are as different as night and day, yet occupy the same time and space. Diametrically opposed, the kingdoms stand in stark opposition to one another, each vying for the citizens of the other and the lesser kingdom posturing itself as supreme. Though both are very real, the citizens of the kingdom of darkness have no idea the other kingdom exists. Some citizens of the kingdom of light are not even aware of the nature of their kingdom. On the surface, it would appear the kingdom of darkness has the advantage over the other, but in reality, the one most visible is doomed already! Its power has been revoked. No outcome other than defeat is available, yet its citizens are deceived by its prince into thinking their kingdom is the only kingdom in existence. The kingdom of God is covert. Unseen and unheralded, its citizens nonetheless represent a kingdom of much greater authority—with much greater power—and a much greater future. Don't get me wrong—it won't always be unseen. At some time designated by God the Father, this kingdom will be established in glory and great visibility, illuminating the whole earth by the presence of Jesus and known by all.

Why do the citizens of the kingdom of this world not hear the citizens of the other kingdom as they proclaim their greater empire? It's quite possibly because the ambassadors proclaiming their "kingdom of light" don't know its scope much better than the people to whom they present it. Though expatriated from the kingdom of darkness to the kingdom of light, remnants of previous loyalties and restrictions still exist in these ambassadors. I personally walked as a citizen of the kingdom of God for many years before I began to recognize the full value of my new citizenship. When a citizen of God's kingdom doesn't believe they have authority, power, and privilege, then they walk in mediocrity as a commoner. It is only when a son of a king knows he is uncommon that he begins to carry himself in an uncommon manner. (Please note: I did not say "in a haughty manner"!)

It is my goal to bring greater "light" in the mind of the reader to the kingdom of light, to give a better understanding of its laws and principles, and to encourage the believer to walk in the citizenship he has been given. Upon discovering the nature of the kingdom, you can begin to seek revelation of it. There is no end to the expounding of understanding and knowledge in the world, but it is the revelation of the kingdom of God that brings freedom. Revelation will not come from this book. Revelation can only come from God. It is my intention to give a description of what you are seeking so you might "seek first the kingdom of God." It is through finding the kingdom of God that He will add "all things" onto you, and revelation from God is what will cause you to find it.

My prayer for you as you read this book is the same as Paul's prayer for the Ephesians:

> *"I keep asking that the God of our Lord Jesus Christ, the glorious Father, may give you the Spirit of wisdom and revelation, so that you may know him better. I pray also that the eyes of your heart may be enlightened in order that you may know the hope to which he has called you, the riches of his glorious inheritance in the saints, and his incomparably great power for us who believe. That power is like the working of his mighty strength, which he exerted in Christ when he raised him from the dead and seated him at his right hand in the heavenly realms, far above all rule and authority, power and dominion, and every title that can be given, not only in the present age but also in the one to come."*
> Ephesians 1:17-21 (NIV)

The revelation of the kingdom is not some new teaching, but rather an old truth Jesus' disciples knew well. Its presence and scope are reflected in the epistles of Paul, who went about preaching the kingdom. During His three and a half year ministry, Jesus often spoke of the kingdom of Heaven in parables. The titles "kingdom of God," "kingdom of Heaven," and "kingdom of Light" were used interchangeably in the kingdom parables and epistles. In this book, unless I indicate that I am relating to Satan's kingdom, any references to "the kingdom" are about God's kingdom. The kingdom has been preached and taught in our times, but many have missed the impact of this message. Still others have thought it to be "pie in the sky for when you die." I hope that this book will help you better understand an old truth, and in the understanding you will begin to seek revelation in a greater way. Has Jesus been "able to do immeasurably more than all you ask or imagine" in your Christian experience? If not, then begin to seek the kingdom, and seek it until you find it!

> *"Again, the kingdom of heaven is like unto a merchant, seeking goodly pearls: Who, when he had found one pearl of great price, went and sold all that he had, and bought it."*
> *Matthew 13:45-46 (KJV)*

Chapter 1
The Fall and Rule of Satan

"No, we speak of God's secret wisdom, a wisdom that has been hidden and that God destined for our glory before time began."
1 Corinthians 2:7 (NIV)

It all began so long ago. He knows the end from the beginning and is never caught by surprise. Let it never be said future events are anything but history to God. Provision was made before the beginning of time for events to come. Before a particle of matter was spoken into existence, before a star was created, before a planet was designed, a plan was devised by the Godhead which would be played out over the ages to deal with the evil that would come. At some point a super being—one of three—was created by God to serve the Godhead. His name was Lucifer.

It is said Lucifer was a worshipper. The accounts of his fall in Isaiah and Ezekiel give us the picture of his purpose and realm. He was called the Day Star, the giver of light. Some believe music was his forte. He was called the Guardian Cherub. So what caused hate to become his delight? How did the "Day Star" become the "Prince of Darkness"? How did the "Guardian Cherub" become "The Spoiler," a killer of infants, a destroyer of life, with one objective: to take what God created and destroy it?

Lucifer served the Godhead with two other mighty angels, Gabriel and Michael. A created being, he was given beauty unsurpassed by any of God's creation. With all the grandeur Lucifer was given, it came into his heart he was equal to God. Pride entered into him. The created began to think himself equal to his creator. He became deceived, as pride deceives all who fall victim to its darkness. Nothing is more blinding than believing what you are is the result of your own efforts, believing that because you have some level of proficiency in a grace in your life, you somehow came upon it by your own power. That you should be the focus of the attention/respect/admiration of someone or everyone because you're you. Whether graced with exceptional intelligence, artistic talent, or fleeting beauty, none of us created our God-given gifts. How then can we take credit for them? Such was the pride of Lucifer, and such was the fuel for his fall.

When Lucifer fell, it did not come as a shock to the King of Kings and the Lord of Lords. Nor did Satan's disruption of God's creation catch its Creator off guard. Though man had not yet been created, God knew what this dark angel would do to man. He also knew what the Son of Man would do to this dark angel.

It is said that when sin was found in Lucifer, he was expelled from heaven. Though stripped of his position, he was still given access to the throne room of God. He took with him a third of the angels, who chose to follow him. However, since the gifts of God are without repentance, Satan, (as he was called on earth), retained his abilities. Cast to the earth and still under the authority of God, Satan was given no rank or privilege except what he took in the form of his authority over his band of rebellious angels. None of his previous glory remained. Any further rank or privilege he sought would have to be achieved through deception, intrigue, and the use of the abilities God created him with. Since he had nothing, Satan would have to steal what he wanted.

God created the earth. He created man and woman to walk as one flesh in fellowship with their Creator and to rule over the planet. God gave Adam the title deed to the whole earth. In reading Genesis, we find that God told Adam the earth and everything in it was his to rule and subdue. God gave him all parts but one—a tree in the middle of the garden. The tree was present as an escape clause to Adam's fellowship with God. At any time, Adam could eat its fruit, so declaring his independence from God. He could always choose death over life. Not much of a choice, you think? Billions are making that same choice today with impunity and with no greater clarity than Adam. But at the start, Adam and Eve walked in grand fellowship with their Lord and God, enjoying unbroken fellowship with Him and each other.

The mortals' fellowship with God was a tough pill to swallow for the one once accustomed to sitting in the presence of God. "How delightful it would be," thought Satan, "to take the objects of God's attention and fellowship, deceive them, and cause God to have to destroy them." Satan would use the consistency of God against God. "I will deceive the woman into distrusting her Creator and choosing sin," he thought to himself. "Adam will probably pick Eve over God, disobeying God's command because of his love for Eve." The title deed to the whole earth rested with Adam, and Satan knew it. "When it is over," Satan chuckled to himself, "Adam and all he rules will become mine. I will have the pleasure of watching God carry out His own death sentence against the ones He loves." In the end, the Devil knew, God would have to carry out the sentence of death Himself, because holy justice would demand it. Satan could count on God being holy in the execution of the sentence. "He is so rigid!" Satan thought to himself, "Never bending—so legalistic! I can count on His boring consistency!"

Chapter 1

Satan prepared his plan well. He would use God's own words to deceive Eve. He would have to twist them a little, but who would notice? Satan knew he was a charmer. He could probably even get Eve to twist the words a little for him. A little exaggeration, a little suggestive interpretation, an appeal to the desire for knowledge, and viola! "It is such a blessing," thought Satan, "God created man with such curiosity! He made it so easy for me!"

Satan's plan couldn't have worked better! Eve ate, and Adam ate, and the rule of Earth passed to Satan.

All of God's created humans now belonged to Satan through Adam. Sin and death had been introduced and would be passed to all earth's inhabitants through Adam. Sin and the death that came with it would separate them from God. The world and all its kingdoms now belonged to Satan. He would eventually offer them to Jesus, the Son of Man, only to be refused, but Satan didn't know that. All Satan knew is he had gained a victory! He didn't have the ability to know the future beyond what God told him. Satan knew how the kingdom of God functioned, how authority worked, and how to deceive. Satan knew he had now become the ruler of the world God had given to man. All its inhabitants, present and future, became his captives. He had won! What Satan didn't know, and couldn't know, was that God had put in place a plan to defeat him long before God ever created this angel who fell.

"How much more intelligent I am than God!" Satan thought. "How much more quick-witted! I am indeed worthy to sit on the throne of the most high God! How I have fooled God," Satan surmised. No one is more deceived than this "Deceiver." How great was his fall, how complete his departure from truth! It is interesting to note that even at this present time the self-proclaimed enemy of the kingdom of God still imagines himself equal to the One who rules even him. Satan's goal remains what it has always been:

Destroy everything of God. Destroy God's creation. Destroy His truth by establishing a lie. Destroy any and all life (which is from God), whether natural or spiritual. Pervert justice and create a counter-culture based on his perversions. Convince the citizens of the kingdom of darkness to believe a lie and oppose the truth. Finally, try to deceive the ambassadors from the kingdom of light into thinking they are powerless to resist Satan, and powerless to enforce the victory already won for them.

> *"For whatever is born of God overcomes the world; and this is the victory that has overcome the world—our faith. Who is the one who overcomes the world, but he who believes that Jesus is the Son of God?"*
> *1 John 5:4-5*

CHAPTER 2
THE LIE

"He was a murderer from the beginning, and does not stand in the truth because there is no truth in him. Whenever he speaks a lie, he speaks from his own nature, for he is a liar and the father of lies."
John 8:44

A lie can only be effective if it is almost indistinguishable from truth. To make a lie work, the liar must present it in such a way as to make the hearer think they are receiving truth and enlightenment. To this end, one laces the lie with sufficient truth to make it appear real, or better yet, enter the lie by degrees while laying sufficient groundwork for it to appear as part of unfolding truth. Deception is an art and a skill, and some are better at it than others. Satan was the author and master of the lie. It was all he had as a weapon, but it was enough. He still uses it with a mastery that lays a trap for many.

The first record we have of the "Master of Deception" at work is in the Garden of Eden. Two things strike me as I consider this account. One; Adam was present during the interaction of his wife and Satan, and two, he never interfered. It's one of those things I intend to ask Adam about when I see him. In the account given in Genesis, we find Satan ignored Adam and related instead to Eve. He began with a question. "Did God really say…?" Doubt is a powerful tool and if the known facts can be brought into question, it prepares the hearer for the deception. Satan's first effort was to try to introduce doubt about what they had heard God say.

The second strategy of the "Father of Lies" was to introduce the idea of self deity and doubt about God's character and motives. Satan said, "For God knows that in the day you eat from it your eyes will be opened, and you will be like God, knowing good and evil." (Genesis 3:5) This was a very clever deception because it did so much in just one statement. First, this lie held up the promise of becoming like God. How exciting! What a delight it would be to be as God was! How much they could know and do! The third part of the lie was the knowledge of good and evil. This had an element of truth to it, but skewed the motives. It is true that the introduction of sin would open the door for knowledge of evil. (They already had knowledge of good but had no comparisons to make.) What wasn't true was that God wanted to have them remain ignorant for the sake of ignorance. Satan wanted them to believe God's nature was such that He would withhold what was good for them to somehow benefit Himself. Satan was trying to make Eve think God had flaws in His character and couldn't be trusted.

Satan's strategy is no different in the workings of the kingdom of darkness today. He is boringly predictable in strategies, but variation is not as important as mastery and he is a master of the lie. "You should be the god of your universe." "Did God say ...?" "Did you really hear and understand what God said?" and, "If God really loved you ..." are the most common lies to enter the heart of those who have decided to commit themselves to God through Christ.

Keep in mind that much of the process to establish these lies has been built into our flesh through reinforced lies as we grew up. These lies have been established by parents, peers, media, and other authority figures. Their influence on our responses require little action by Satan. Our flesh—the combination of mind and body—propagates the lies for Satan, having been reinforced in us by a kingdom he controls. I will more clearly develop this for you in later chapters.

In response to the first lie, why should you be the god of your own universe? You didn't create 'you.' You were created by a living being who has full knowledge of whom and what you are. The Lord, the Creator, created you by design with purpose. However, the kingdom of darkness has tried to assault this concept with absolute vehemence. Satan introduced the concept of "birth by chance" through Darwin, and the world (looking for a reason to not be accountable to a creator) grabbed onto this lie with fervor. Evolution began to be taught in our schools as "good science" though it was neither well thought out nor could it be called "science." There are many good books written which expose the lies of evolution and if you still cling to this old lie, please take the time to become informed and abandon it. You were created. You have responsibilities to the Creator and you will stand before the Lord and give an account. Anyone or any thought which tells you different is a lie. Take it captive and get rid of it!

> *"We are destroying speculations and every lofty thing raised up against the knowledge of God, and we are taking every thought captive to the obedience of Christ."*
> 2 Corinthians 10:5

The second lie, "Did God really say ...?" is meant to cause you to turn back from the course which is set before you. Your mind will begin to question the directions God has given you. We have the bible, and we can research the standard direction which God gives everyone, but until you know what the Word of God says, Satan can seriously confuse you. Have you noticed how hard it is to study God's word? Why do you suppose that is? I believe one reason is that when we learn God's word, we will become responsible to it. Our flesh resists this responsibility so we don't discipline ourselves as we should. Another reason, however, is if we really understand who we are in Christ, we become a viable threat to the kingdom of darkness, so our enemy doesn't want us to ever understand it. I believe we meet spiritual resistance to reading God's word. The strategy to counter the lie, "Did God really say ..." is to begin to discipline yourself to read God's word and to understand the truth in it. Watch how men of God interpret the scriptures and present its truths. Study to show yourself approved, rightly interpreting the word of God (II Timothy 2:15). If God speaks to you in His still small voice, giving direction which is specific to you, make certain to keep a journal of what God said to you. List the circumstances and the evidence which let you know it was from God. There will come many trials and testing in God's plan for your life, and you will need to have all the weapons you can muster to refute the lies of the enemy. When the enemy whispers "Did God really say ...?" read your journal and say out loud to the doubts screaming at you in your mind "This IS what my God has said!" It is in the "rhema" (proceeding) word of God which you will be most tested, and it is important you are not dissuaded from God's kingdom plan for you. Stand ready to fight the doubts which will come.

The third lie I want to look at is "If God really loved you ..." Satan gets believers to doubt their Creator and their Savior. He points out times God could have supposedly delivered us but didn't. The deceiver makes a case for bad circumstances and points to God as the guilty party. "If God really loved you" is a common phrase in the lies he weaves. Simply asking the questions raises a level of doubt and the most insidious part is Satan will reference evil which he has brought against you and then use it to accuse God of neglect. The statement Satan should make, if stated honestly should be, "If God really loved you would He have allowed me to work this evil into your life?" Of course, stated that way it highlights the fact the enemy only gets the authority he can steal and has no real power.

God does allow evil to come close to us in certain circumstances. This has always been difficult for Christians to understand, even with the book of Job as a reference. Why does evil come? Why are we not always "delivered from evil"? These are valid questions which sometimes hang there with no valid response. God won't always deliver us and won't always tell us why. This gives the enemy the power behind the argument he uses to discourage us and attack our faith. Part of the reason for our vulnerability to such an attack is a misunderstanding of both the nature of our God and our nature. God's thoughts are far above our thoughts. He sees the end from the beginning. We can't possibly understand the whole picture. If a parent has a six year old and tells him, "No, you can't have another cookie," or, "No, you can't stay up until midnight," it will seem to the child that their loving parents are tyrants who are not to be trusted. Even as they grow into adolescence they are not able to understand the restrictive nature of their good parents. A child's frame of reference is so limited they cannot understand why the discomfort is actually good for them.

This similarity in a limited frame of reference is what causes the enemy to be able to make a case for his lie. "If God really loved you, wouldn't He give you what you want and not cause you the heartache of being deprived of what you desired?" This argument picks up greater steam the larger the sacrifice. "If God really cared about you, He wouldn't have taken your child before their time. If God cared, He wouldn't have let you lose your job and experience all sorts of financial hardship." And so the enemy's arguments go.

In the midst of all the trials Christians face, we must remember that God has put in place a function which guarantees a good outcome, if we remember its parameters. "ALL things work together for good (and don't miss these parameters) for those that love the Lord and are called according to His purposes." (Romans 8:28)

Our biggest problem is that we are committed to our own purposes. The enemy hits us where it hurts and we are committed to not hurting. However, if we surrender our purposes to God's, He turns it around on the deceiver. What Satan intends for harm brings forth the advance of God's kingdom and God lets us have the reward.

Jesus didn't leave us without knowledge. He said, "In the world you will have tribulation, but take courage; I have overcome the world." (John 16:33) Yes, things will hurt. Yes, Christians will experience disappointment. But through it all, God will work His purpose and the outcome will be worth the cost.

Part of the confusion Christians experience is the tendency to think that God's reason for being is to give us what we want. He is a big sugar daddy in the sky who will bless our socks off if we will just believe Him for it. They define "faith in God" as "faith God will give us all our heart's desire." That is not what constitutes faith, though it has often been presented that way. We have hearts infected with sin and lack the foresight to really understand the best thing for ourselves. Faith is the total acceptance that God will give you the best possible outcome in a sinful fallen world Satan controls, and the outcome will have such eternal significance we can accept any hardship of the moment. Trusting God is simply trusting God—not trusting God for a given outcome. Job's response was "Though He slay me yet will I trust Him". (Job 13:15) If you develop Job's strategy, then the lies of the enemy don't move you away from God, but toward God. We seek the Lord for the strength to endure and to persevere and the outcome purchases for us a better eternity.

Counting your trials as a blessing is a practice encouraged by both James and Peter in the epistles. The fact is, trials are indeed blessings! They are not reasons to doubt God! Everything we do and overcome is on record and will be used to reward or not. All of our trials work for us (2 Corinthians 4:17) a far greater glory and we can be confident in the word of Paul who wrote, "For I consider that the sufferings of this present time are not worthy to be compared with the glory that is to be revealed to us." (Romans 8:18)

A man I knew shared a dream the Lord had given him. I share it with you now. I believe his dream was from God and the experience changed the way he looked at life and responded to it.

The Two Rooms

In my dream, I died and found myself immediately with Jesus, as the word of God said we would. Jesus took me by the hand and led me with him into heaven. At that point, I could not tell I was dreaming. As far as I knew, I had indeed died and was now with the Lord for eternity.

"Welcome, my friend," Jesus said to me as He walked up and put his arm around my shoulders. "I have awaited this moment with eagerness. As my word told you, each person must give an account, and before you do, I have two rooms we must visit."

I walked on a little with Jesus and we came to a door with a sign which said "Rewards."

"This is the room of rewards." Jesus said, "It is here I will show you those things you did in your life. These are things which laid up for yourself great treasures for all eternity—treasures I will give you. But before we go there, we must first visit this next room."

We walked a bit further and came to another door. The sign on that door said "Regrets" and I wondered what we would find there. I apprehensively walked through the door and into the room behind Jesus. He motioned me to a seat facing a wall and sat down next to me. As I watched, the wall in front of me seemed to disappear and I looked into a scene which was unfolding before me almost as a movie but in this case a three dimensional movie as if I was there. In the first scene, I saw a man talking to someone I knew as Harold, a man from my home town whom was someone of great influence in our community. As a result of the conversation between the two, this man was brought into the presence of great men and what turned out later to be great events. Everything led to the next and as a rock thrown into a pond, the ripples went out to touch hundreds and then thousands. This man, who must have been a great man, intrigued me. I saw his influence cause many to come to the Lord.

Chapter 2

As I watched, Jesus came to this man and put his arm around his shoulders as he had mine when we first met and motioned to a huge multitude of people. He told him, "These are all here because of your obedience."

"Who is he?" I asked the Lord and Jesus directed me back to the scene. As I watched, the scene drew close to the man's face and I was shocked to see it was me.

"But I didn't do any of those things I saw him do!" I protested.

"I know," Jesus said sadly. "You chose a different outcome, and as a result there are those whose rewards are greater than yours. But I needed to show you what I had planned for your life—my good, acceptable, and perfect will for your life—so you would know I did not neglect you. I prepare a place for each of you in your world, but every man can choose. The outcome of your life is in your hands. You can choose my will or you can choose your will. Before I show you the rewards I am able to give you, I needed to show you I had not chosen a lesser outcome for you than others. I had destined you for much but you chose less."

Then I remembered the day I was to have met with Harold, but instead I went fishing with my buddies. I knew the Lord had told me to go, but it had seemed more important to do what I had wanted that day. Scene after scene showed me outcome after outcome which could have been mine, would have been mine, should have been mine, but I chose otherwise.

I watched the world in the wall as the video of my life was displayed before me. I saw myself in the circumstances of my day-to-day decisions and watched those times I chose to indulge myself. I saw those times I chose my will over His will for my life. The times I was too filled with unbelief to do the things that God was asking. I saw the times I went for the money and what I would eat and what I would wear rather than the things of God's kingdom. He showed me those times I was too self absorbed to even hear the master's voice. I looked on and saw the times my own pleasure became more important than His kingdom. I saw those times I decided to make truth irrelevant and left the light of His word to dabble in the grays of the world. I saw the choices I made which were non-biblical. I watched those times when the pleasures of the moment seemed more desirable than the pleasures of the kingdom of heaven. In my heart I felt the weight of the loss and I saw in Jesus' countenance how sad He was that what He created me to have and to be, was thrown away by me at the moments of choice. I felt his disappointment. It was not disapproval or disappointment in me. I could see that. It was disappointment He would now have to give me less than He had wanted to give me—less than a parent would want for their child. The tears which fell in that room were His.

I don't really know how long we sat there, but it ended and as we got up to go I remembered the verse in Corinthians which said, "If any man's work is burned up, he will suffer loss; but he himself will be saved, yet so as through fire." It felt like fire in my heart and I felt the loss my bad choices had taken from me. I wondered what would be left to show me in the 'reward room' since I had thrown away so much.

Jesus' face seemed lighter and so peaceful and eager as we entered the next room. We sat again looking at a wall which became scenes from the life I had just left. I felt an instant disappointment as I watched, for it seemed all that was being shown were such mundane and lackluster moments of insignificance.

One scene was a moment when I rifled through the console of my car to give a homeless guy a few quarters. "What's that got to do with rewards?" I asked Jesus. "I only had about 75 cents."

"Oh, there's no reward for the money," Jesus said. "The reward I give you will be for the smile and the comment you made to him. You said what I put in your heart to say. "Don't give up buddy," you told him. You see, I didn't bring him across your path for the money, but for the kind word. He was despondent and was getting ready to kill himself, and he wanted the money for a bus trip to the bridge to jump. If you had enough for his bus fare, I wouldn't have let him find you, but I knew the kindness you would show in your smile would save his life. What he saw in you gave him hope and he came through that dark time and served me faithfully throughout the rest of his life. He has impacted many and you will share his rewards with him."

Then there was the waitress who spilled my supper all over me in a business meeting. It was one of those rare instances when I responded to her discomfort more than my discomfort, and the Lord showed me what had been going on in her life with her children and their father, and how my single act of kindness encouraged her in her trials. How it gave her courage to keep going.

"As you did to her, so you did to me," Jesus said. "This moment also has its own reward."

As I watched, each seemingly insignificant act of kindness, each minor victory blossomed into a full bouquet and this time the tears which fell were mine. How little I had done, yet how great was the reward as my Lord took each and touched it with His love and caused it to grow into something great.

"Wow! I never even knew," I told Jesus, as I watched all of these simple things which had been part of my life become so beautiful with but a touch of Jesus' hand. "But surely these have earned me no great reward. I put so little effort into them."

"It is not the effort of you which makes you great," Jesus said, "but the presence of me in you. Those things can only happen when the 'you' is absent in you. These scenes I have showed you were the times you let go of you and I was free to use you as a tool."

"I feel such unworthiness," I told the Lord. "You saw all the bad choices I made my whole life and yet you took what little I offered and it has brought such great return! How? Why?"

"I have loved you," was Jesus response, "As I had Paul write in my word, you have been made heirs of God and fellow heirs with Christ, if indeed you suffer with Him so that you may also be glorified with Him. These words are true and will come to pass for you, but your time is not now. You have yet more exploits. And lo I am with you always, even unto the end of the earth."

I awoke and found myself still in my bed, in my home, on this earth, and with choices that still lay ahead of me. My prayer from that day forward was that I would choose always the things the Lord had in mind for me and with what was left of my life, I would indeed "seek first the Kingdom of God."

Satan knows he can't destroy you. He knows he can't defeat you. His only hope is to try to dissuade you from the truth, slow you down, make you ineffective, encourage you to make bad choices, and spoil the blessings that God has for you. The Deceiver tries to convince you that your flesh and the immediate needs you feel have greater relevance than the kingdom. In doing so, he tries to keep you from choosing your destiny. He tries to keep you from reaching your potential in the kingdom. When the enemy speaks, it's all a lie and he knows it. But he's good at it, and Satan in his heart actually believes he will defeat the truth with his lies. How deceived pride has made him!

> *"You are of your father the devil, and you want to do the desires of your father. He was a murderer from the beginning, and does not stand in the truth because there is no truth in him. Whenever he speaks a lie, he speaks from his own nature, for he is a liar and the father of lies."*
> John 8:44

Chapter 3
The Announcement
"The kingdom is in your midst!"

Now in those days John the Baptist came, preaching in the wilderness of Judea, saying, "Repent, for the kingdom of heaven is at hand."
Matthew 3:1-2

"The kingdom of God is at hand"! The people of Israel had been waiting so very long for that message. Many had given up hope it would come in their lifetime. "A king again! National recognition which went beyond that of an occupied colony! What an excitement! This would establish Israel again as a sovereign nation!" they thought.

So long Israel had awaited the message that I am sure many had decided it probably wasn't going to come anytime soon. Not in any time frame which would affect them and their families anyway. When they did entertain the thought, it was with the idea their present ruler, Rome, would be dramatically removed from their land. This was a message people longed to hear, but had little idea what it really meant to them.

Consider how much emphasis was put on the message of the kingdom during that time. It was the main message and central to the theme of Jesus' ministry.

When John the Baptist came on the scene, it was the first message he addressed.

"Repent, for the kingdom of heaven is at hand."
Matthew 3:2

Chapter 3

Jesus came bringing the same message:

From that time Jesus began to preach and say, "Repent, for the kingdom of heaven is at hand."
Matthew 4:17

Jesus was going throughout all Galilee, teaching in their synagogues and proclaiming the gospel of the kingdom, and healing every kind of disease and every kind of sickness among the people.
Matthew 4:23

Then He sent out His disciples to preach the same message:

These twelve Jesus sent out after instructing them: "And as you go, preach, saying, 'The kingdom of heaven is at hand.'"
Matthew 10:5, 7

John, Jesus, and His disciples were three witnesses that the kingdom of heaven was the message of the day, each declaring, "The kingdom of heaven is at hand." Now this brings a question to mind; is "the kingdom of heaven is at hand" a promise for about 2000 years later or does "at hand" mean it's at hand? Does it only exist in heaven or is it supposed to be in our midst? Was Jesus' instruction to pray "Your kingdom come" supposed to address a time centuries down the road? There are differing opinions about this, but the general consensus of the preaching I hear in the United States is that the kingdom of heaven only happens when we get to heaven. This is an unfortunate consensus. I believe it has caused many to ignore their inheritance. They think of it as only for another time and place, and while they are here they should "do as the Romans do." The standard message preached has been predominantly the gospel of salvation as it refers to your eternity. While a valid enough message, I think focusing solely on a message which points to the hereafter decentralizes the Christian experience and gives a promise and a hope for the after life, while ignoring the power of today. The disciples did not go out preaching the gospel of salvation, but the gospel of the kingdom. Frankly, the kingdom message is much bigger than just our salvation, though salvation is certainly an important part of it. It is our salvation experience which makes a way for us to see the kingdom. Salvation is required since the kingdom must be spiritually discerned.

> *Jesus answered and said to him, "Truly, truly, I say to you, unless one is born again he cannot see the kingdom of God."*
> *John 3:3*

The fallen state of man does not allow him to see the kingdom of heaven as it exists in this world today. He can only see what his natural eyes can see. The things of God are spiritually discerned and the bible tells us they cannot be understood by the natural mind. Only through Jesus when we get saved, or "born again," are we given the spiritual presence of God within us which allows us to perceive His kingdom in our midst.

> *But the natural man does not receive the things of the Spirit of God, for they are foolishness to him; nor can he know them, because they are spiritually discerned.*
> *1 Corinthians 2:14 (NKJV)*

> *And the disciples came and said to Him, "Why do you speak to them in parables?" Jesus answered them, "To you it has been granted to know the mysteries of the kingdom of heaven, but to them it has not been granted."*
> *Matthew 13:10-11*

Chapter 3

This discernment was not present in the Pharisees. They saw only their own religiosity and I believe were not open to revelation from the Spirit. The religious leaders of that day were so set on the concept of a natural visible kingdom it prompted them to ask Jesus a question which showed their ignorance.

Now having been questioned by the Pharisees as to when the kingdom of God was coming, He answered them and said, "The kingdom of God is not coming with signs to be observed; nor will they say, 'Look, here it is!' or, 'There it is!' For behold, the kingdom of God is in your midst."
Luke 17:20-21

What a strong statement that was! It tells me there is a kingdom of God coming into its own that very moment. It doesn't sound like Jesus is speaking of the sweet by and by. It also doesn't sound like He is saying it won't happen until His second coming. As further evidence the kingdom was very near to being established, Jesus concluded one of His talks on the cost of discipleship with the following statement:

"But I say to you truthfully, there are some of those standing here who will not taste death until they see the kingdom of God."
Luke 9:27

That simple statement has caused theologians some real biblical crowbarring in an effort to try to get it to fit their doctrine. Try this interpretation on for size. Jesus knew that when he was crucified, his death would make a way for the Holy Spirit to reside in the believers themselves, and the kingdom would be available for everyone willing to accept His sacrifice. His disciples would be equipped to spread the gospel of the kingdom with power. They would do even greater works than He had done. There were certain lifestyle changes which would be required and not all those He was speaking to would make the changes before they died, but many would. They would be able to see the kingdom of God established with power as the Holy Spirit filled them in Jerusalem, and Samaria and the uttermost parts of the earth. The message would be spread with power throughout the known and eventually the unknown world. I believe this represents a much more believable idea and requires no interpretational gymnastics to force it to fit the message Jesus preached. When it comes to biblical interpretation, one should take the path of least resistance. If an interpretation causes problems, rethink the interpretation. There are no conflicted scriptures, just conflicted theologians.

There are certain requirements of kingdom living, which I will talk about in greater detail later. Many believers saw the kingdom and its requirements, changed their citizenship and moved into it. Many didn't. I think it is the many who didn't, who eventually caused a large part of the Church to come up with all sorts of reasons why the power of the kingdom was only for 'back then' and not for today. Eventually that non-Biblical position became widely accepted. However, there is simply no legitimate way to warp scripture to fit your theology or the popular theology of the day. For example, some believers say that spiritual gifts aren't for today; they were just for biblical times. This is completely unbiblical. It causes an unfortunate rejection of the power God has given His people to use in fulfilling His calling on their lives.

If you are a believer walking carnally amongst Christians who are walking by the Spirit, there will be considerable difference in the level of power in your walk and testimony and considerable difference in God's presence in your life. What better way to excuse the lack of anointing in your walk than to declare it was only for another time and now most normal Christians can't have that power? "Oh, of course God still does His occasional miracle," they add, "but it's nothing you should come to expect in a normal Christian experience."

Chapter 3

I have a saying: "If your experience doesn't match the scriptures, keep the scriptures and throw out your experience!" In other words, "Let God be true and every man a liar!" (Romans 3:4) There are many reasons given for no power. While these reasons prove helpful for excusing the lacks of the teller, it is not the message of the kingdom. The message of the kingdom is this:

> *"The Law and the Prophets were proclaimed until John; since that time the gospel of the kingdom of God has been preached, and everyone is forcing his way into it."*
> Luke 16:16

> *"I tell you the truth: Among those born of women there has not risen anyone greater than John the Baptist; yet he who is least in the kingdom of heaven is greater than he. From the days of John the Baptist until now, the kingdom of heaven has been forcefully advancing, and forceful men lay hold of it. For all the Prophets and the Law prophesied until John. And if you are willing to accept it, he is the Elijah who was to come."*
> Matthew 11:11-14

> *"Truly, truly, I say to you, he who believes in Me, the works that I do, he will do also; and greater works than these he will do; because I go to the Father. Whatever you ask in My name, that will I do, so that the Father may be glorified in the Son. If you ask Me anything in My name, I will do it."*
> John 14:12-14

It is interesting that Jesus relates to the power for the believer as being greater in the least of those of the kingdom than in John, whom He proclaimed was the greatest of the prophets. There is much in the Bible about the power of the believer. Yet when we consider the state of the average believer, we can only suppose that perhaps the truth of things is not being completely presented, because huge portions of the body of Christ don't walk in these truths. The kingdom is meant to be a place of power for your Christian walk. It is the power of God moving through and in you to advance the kingdom of God here in this dark, desolate planet. The kingdom is in your midst; it's inside of you if you have the Holy Spirit. But, it is advancing itself outside of you as you fulfill God's purpose for your life.

What about those who don't find the power of the kingdom of God to be their Christian experience? I believe many Christians never enter into the kingdom and won't until it comes with great visibility at the return of Christ at their resurrection. I believe there are a couple of reasons for this. One is that they never come to a clear understanding of the kingdom. Either they never hear the message of the kingdom or when they do, the enemy takes the understanding away. Jesus gives the parable of the sower and the resulting lack of fruit.

> *"When anyone hears the word of the kingdom and does not understand it, the evil one comes and snatches away what has been sown in his heart. This is the one on whom seed was sown beside the road."*
> Matthew 13:19

Another reason for not pursuing the kingdom is that the requirements of kingdom living demand a 24/7 experience with Christ. No, I am not saying you should quit your job and let your hair grow and wander in the desert. However, you the believer are to be in the world and not of the world. You don't do the same things. You don't define your life the same way. You don't measure success with the same parameters. You don't spend your free time the same way. You don't enjoy all the same activities or live according to worldly principles. You demonstrate godly character. You measure yourself (not those of this world) by a different standard and you don't settle for the same standards as a non-Christian.

Chapter 3

Jesus spent a good portion of His ministry trying to establish what constituted the life of a disciple and kingdom citizenship. He told many parables about what constituted kingdom living. He spoke about how to enter the kingdom of God and what would keep one out. If you only think about the kingdom as an after death experience, it makes the concept of His parables very difficult to understand. What in the world was Jesus talking about in His parables? What does He mean when He referenced deeds, when He says, "Some enter in and some do not"? Isn't salvation a free gift purchased by Christ for those who will accept it? Of course it is! Paul's writings gave us no doubt about that. It is of grace and not of works. He was very clear. But it is not the cost of salvation which is in question here, but the cost of discipleship—kingdom citizenship. You can live your entire existence here on earth, die and still enter heaven having never once entered into the kingdom of God as it functions here on earth. If you start from that position, things make a little more sense.

Please know however, this non-kingdom experience is not the "good, perfect, and acceptable" plan of God for your life. He has gone to prepare a place for you according to what your response is here. He calls you to citizenship and gives to you the keys to the kingdom. It is a lifestyle here, as well as in eternity that He purchased for you, but He leaves it up to you how you move into it. According to the Bible, there is a better resurrection for those that choose it (Hebrews 11:35). For this end of the age, the difference can be even more dramatic as many of Jesus' parables show.

How then do you enter into the kingdom of God here on this earth? Well, let's look at what Jesus had to say about this subject.

"But seek first His kingdom and His righteousness, and all these things will be added to you."
Matthew 6:33

His message was clear. The natural things of this world are not supposed to be the focus of a Christian. We are supposed to leave those concerns in the hands of our Father who knows our needs even before we ask. (Note: we are still encouraged to ask.) He gives each person a purpose in this world and He will equip the person for that purpose, both naturally and spiritually.

While seeking His kingdom first, ahead of all of your other worldly pursuits is necessary, seeking His righteousness is even more necessary. He tells the crowds,

> "Enter through the narrow gate; for the gate is wide and the way is broad that leads to destruction, and there are many who enter through it. For the gate is small and the way is narrow that leads to life, and there are few who find it.
>
> "Beware of the false prophets, who come to you in sheep's clothing, but inwardly are ravenous wolves. You will know them by their fruits. Grapes are not gathered from thorn bushes nor figs from thistles, are they? So every good tree bears good fruit, but the bad tree bears bad fruit. A good tree cannot produce bad fruit, nor can a bad tree produce good fruit. Every tree that does not bear good fruit is cut down and thrown into the fire. So then, you will know them by their fruits. Not everyone who says to Me, 'Lord, Lord,' will enter the kingdom of heaven, but he who does the will of My Father who is in heaven will enter. Many will say to Me on that day, 'Lord, Lord, did we not prophesy in Your name, and in Your name cast out demons, and in Your name perform many miracles?' And then I will declare to them, 'I never knew you; depart from me you who practice lawlessness.'"
> Matthew 7:13-23

Chapter 3

"Not everyone who says to Me, 'Lord, Lord,' will enter the kingdom of heaven, but he who does the will of My Father who is in heaven will enter," Jesus says, "It is the one who does the will of my father who enters." It is in the doing, that citizenship is established. Religiosity is not the key. Knowing Jesus is Lord is not the key. Knowing Jesus as Lord is the key. It is doing what He tells you to do. It is obedience to His commands. It is the acceptance of His will over your own. There are many Christians I know who get all excited about Jesus but don't get excited at all about what He wants. They proclaim Him a great Prophet, Teacher and Savior but neglect His commands—or simply think of them as suggestions. Many of them call Him Lord, but don't walk with Him as Lord. Kingdom living is about obedience, and it is those who obey Him that enter.

Is Jesus addressing an after death entrance to the kingdom of heaven in Matthew 7:23 when He says, "Depart from me you who practice lawlessness?" If so, the statement about "doing" earlier in the passage flies in the face of a doctrine of "salvation by grace and not of works" (Ephesians 2:9). Jesus is not ignorant about the basis of salvation. He is not saying your eternity depends on your ability to function within a set of rules or responses. I believe He is simply stating that those who call Him Lord but don't give Him Lordship will not be able to enter the kingdom of God as it exists here on this planet. There is no other interpretation which maintains consistency with the basis of salvation as presented by Paul in the Letter to the Ephesians, not to mention all the other "salvation by grace" scriptures.

Many times Jesus addressed the concept of trying to maintain two citizenships or trying to live both kingdoms at once. His call for disciples produced many who wanted to follow him—someday.

And He said to another, "Follow Me." But he said, "Lord, permit me first to go and bury my father." But He said to him, "Allow the dead to bury their own dead; but as for you, go and proclaim everywhere the kingdom of God." Another also said, "I will follow You, Lord; but first permit me to say goodbye to those at home." But Jesus said to him, "No one, after putting his hand to the plow and looking back, is fit for the kingdom of God."
Luke 9:59-62

Jesus left little doubt that the kingdom came first. The kingdom is forward looking and you can't hold on to what was before and still obtain what is to be. There was no excuse good enough to replace the kingdom, and when Jesus spoke of it, it was in conjunction with surrendering yourself and all your efforts.

He spoke of how hard it was for the rich to enter the kingdom:

And Jesus looked at him and said, "How hard it is for those who are wealthy to enter the kingdom of God! For it is easier for a camel to go through the eye of a needle than for a rich man to enter the kingdom of God."
Luke 18:24-25

The rich young man who approached Jesus had asked about eternal life—"Zoe" spiritual life of the kingdom. He was told to sell all he had and follow Jesus, but he was unable to because he had many possessions, Jesus used that incident to speak on how difficult it is to be rich and kingdom-minded at the same time.

This scripture embodies many of the problems I see in Christianity in the United States. Much of what I see labeled as Christianity seems disturbingly like what Jesus spoke about to the church in Laodicea. Even the poor in this country are rich compared to the poor in most of the world, and our average citizen is richer than nine-tenths of the rest of the world including their rich. I find this makes it very hard for Christians in this country to enter the kingdom of God in this life. They would rather depend on their riches to give them what they want.

Another qualification Jesus gave for entering into the kingdom was His call to be childlike in our acceptance of our Father's love and authority.

> *But Jesus called for them, saying, "Permit the children to come to Me, and do not hinder them, for the kingdom of God belongs to such as these. Truly I say to you, whoever does not receive the kingdom of God like a child will not enter it at all."*
> Luke 18:16-17

"Like a child." What exactly does He mean here? I believe He is speaking of a walk that relies totally on the Father and not on our own understanding. It is not for children to set their own course. They go where their parents go. When they have a need they don't run around trying to solve it. They go to their parent and ask them to solve it. If their parent says "No," they accept the "No." When their parent blesses them, they receive it with joy, not with the presumption it was theirs anyway and they're only getting what they deserve. When they rise in the morning they believe anything could happen that day and go about the day looking for their next adventure. They have wants but they learn to submit those wants to their parents. It is that mind set which allows a Christian to enter the kingdom of God in their Christian experience. I believe this is what He is speaking about here.

In the chapters ahead we will look more closely at the process you go through that causes you to enter the kingdom of God in your Christian experience. You will have a chance to get an understanding of what designates citizenship and how the kingdom of God/Heaven functions here and now in this world. For now though, the coming of Jesus ushered in the age of the Spirit and with His resurrection the kingdom of Heaven had arrived on this earth with power.

The announcement was made, "The kingdom of heaven is at hand." The kingdom was at hand, and Jesus spent His 3½ year ministry preaching the gospel of the kingdom. His message was one of hope and excitement and was given to those who were willing to accept it. The religious leaders of the day mostly refused it, because it removed the power from the hands of the leaders, and placed it in the hands of all the people who would seek the kingdom. It is a kingdom whose glory belongs only to the Lord. It is about Him and His power and not about us. Many refused it. Will you?

"But seek His kingdom, and these things will be added to you. Do not be afraid, little flock, for your Father has chosen gladly to give you the kingdom."
Luke 12:31-32

CHAPTER 4
The Defeat of the Prince of Darkness

"Therefore when Jesus had received the sour wine, He said, "It is finished!" And He bowed His head and gave up His spirit."
John 19:30

At this declaration, "It is finished!" Satan's demise was assured. All authority in heaven and earth would now become Christ's. The work He had come to perform was accomplished. The debt for the earth was paid. The will of His Father was fulfilled. The enemy was defeated. From this time forward, the dead in Christ would go immediately to be with the Lord.

"These are in accordance with the working of the strength of His might which He brought about in Christ, when He raised Him from the dead and seated Him at His right hand in the heavenly places, far above all rule and authority and power and dominion, and every name that is named, not only in this age but also in the one to come."
Ephesians 1:19-21

"For since by a man came death, by a man also came the resurrection of the dead. For as in Adam all die, so also in Christ all will be made alive. But each in his own order: Christ the first fruits, after that those who are Christ's at His coming, then comes the end, when He hands over the kingdom to the God and Father, when He has abolished all rule and all authority and power. For He must reign until He has put all His enemies under His feet. The last enemy that will be abolished is death. For He has put all things in subjection under His feet. But when He says, 'All things are put in subjection,' it is evident that He is excepted who put all things in subjection to Him.

When all things are subjected to Him, then the Son Himself also will be subjected to the One who subjected all things to Him, so that God may be all in all."
1 Corinthians 15:21-28

"When you were dead in your transgressions and the uncircumcision of your flesh, He made you alive together with Him, having forgiven us all our transgressions, having canceled out the certificate of debt consisting of decrees against us, which was hostile to us; and He has taken it out of the way, having nailed it to the cross. When He had disarmed the rulers and authorities, He made a public display of them, having triumphed over them through Him."
Colossians 2:13-15

It is evident that Satan cannot see the outcome of events and must only surmise what will happen next. Had he known how things would turn out, I'm sure he would not have done what he did to Jesus. His strategy has always been flawed, but then sin is the killer of pure thought. He is rebellious enough to disregard the laws of God, and seeing his move against Jesus, I doubt he even understood the legal ramifications of a sinless sacrifice. Even as intelligent as Satan is, sin pollutes his thinking and causes him to overestimate his own intellect. Take note here! It is a weakness which exists in us all. We must guard against it. James points it out:

Come now, you who say, "Today or tomorrow we will go to such and such a city, and spend a year there and engage in business and make a profit." Yet you do not know what your life will be like tomorrow. You are just a vapor that appears for a little while and then vanishes away. Instead, you ought to say, "If the Lord wills, we will live and also do this or that." But as it is, you boast in your arrogance; all such boasting is evil.
James 4:13-16

Satan's plans came to an abrupt proverbial brick wall at the crucifixion of Christ. All of Satan's efforts to thwart the living God were repulsed and he lost! He is a defeated foe and has no real power. He is all smoke and mirrors and what he gets now from God's people, he gets by deception. In order to understand fully the defeat of Satan and what it means and how it was accomplished, you must understand the concept of universal physical and spiritual law. Law is part of the government of things. It is not a bad word or something to be done away with. Jesus said He came to fulfill the law, not to do away with the law. The old law would be fulfilled by a greater law, purchased by blood. Salvation no longer would be by law—though it really never was—but by grace. Most of the laws of the universe would still remain in place. Has salvation by grace suddenly made all other laws irrelevant? The obvious answer is, "No!"

I have two points I want to make:

1. The laws of God are eternal and were not thrown out at any time, including at the death and resurrection of Jesus. They can, however, be counteracted by higher laws.

First, let's consider moral law. Though Jesus' death set free those who choose to rely on His death and moved us into the laws of grace, it is still not acceptable to steal. Parts of the laws which were not fulfilled by Jesus in His ministry and death are still valid. Adultery is still wrong. If you murder someone, you have still done a bad thing. Coveting is not considered a good thing. Being disobedient to parents is still not permissible. Though society is trying its hardest to overthrow the moral laws, they are still relevant to man and even more so for those who belong to the Lord.

A perfect example is an article I read written by a sadly misinformed news reporter. While writing about the fact that more men and women are "uniting" outside of marriage than within marriage, the reporter argued that we could no longer consider marriage "moral." If the majority didn't agree, it couldn't be morally wrong to enjoy a benefit of marriage without the commitment. What a concept! Morality by majority! The reporter obviously doesn't understand laws and how they work. Would murder become acceptable if we all started doing it? I don't think so. However, since Satan does not want society to be responsible to God's order, there is always public pressure to overthrow it. Even in the Christian community, saints loudly proclaim their liberty from the law and declare grace means authority within the church is no longer relevant. This move is NOT from God. While we are under grace, this does not mean we are no longer under laws or government. It also does not mean the price Jesus paid overthrew all existing laws.

Let's consider the laws of physics. Has grace replaced the law of inertia? The second law of thermodynamics might be ignored by the big bang proponents, but that doesn't mean it has stopped functioning. Look at the lemmings which migrate to their death in the Artic. At a point in time they all disregard the law of gravity and fall to their death over a bluff into the sea. The law of gravity can't simply be done away with by having the majority ignore it. No, the physical laws of the universe are still functioning. Jesus didn't do away with those laws at His coming. All of them are needed and firmly in place.

Part of the problem is that some people see "law" as a bad thing. Laws are simply rules of behavior designed by God. Most of our good worldly social laws have been based upon concepts established by God, or at least by those who saw the benefit of functioning in a way which promoted social well being, which is what laws are meant to do. God's moral law is said to be summed up in "Love the Lord your God" and "Love your neighbor as yourself". If followed, they cause interaction and social fabric to be strengthened and problems to be absent. Laws have been put in place to allow us to continue living and enjoying the life we are living.

2. The universe—spiritual and physical—functions within an establish framework of law.

Laws by their nature define the universe and how the parts of the universe interact with one another. To understand how spiritual laws work, we need to look deeper into some of the physical laws. For example, an airplane can overcome the law of gravity by making use of the laws of aerodynamics. The laws of aerodynamics don't remove the law of gravity. It remains firmly in place functioning as it was meant to. It's a good thing too, or the airplane wouldn't be able to land. By making use of both laws, the airplane reaches its destination and lands safely on the ground. After an extensive flight with the laws of aerodynamics setting the plane free from the laws of gravity, it utilizes the law of gravity in order to return to the ground from the sky. It must create a balance between the two to keep from landing too harshly.

The spiritual kingdom has similar application of laws; it has laws which overshadow or set Christians free from lower laws. For example, Romans 8:2 tells us "the law of the Spirit of life in Christ Jesus has set you free from the law of sin and of death." The law of sin and death still remains, but just as the laws of aerodynamics sets the airplane free from the law of gravity, Christ, by His sinless death, established a higher law which functions to set the Christian free from the law of sin and death—provided of course, you make use of it. If the airplane remains stationary, the law of gravity remains in effect and all of the laws of aerodynamics in the world won't get it off the ground, but when the plane moves forward, it can begin to make use of the laws of aerodynamics. If a Christian remains rooted in their former lifestyle, the laws of sin and death keep functioning and he or she remain firmly in the blues of Romans 7, caught in the grip of the laws of sin and death. It is only as they act on their new freedom, the higher law begins to counter the base law and they are set free from the law of sin and death. This process of being set free is not automatic. It happens by design and purpose, just like the airplane taking off. A Christian must determine which law will dominate in their life.

> *"For those who are according to the flesh set their minds on the things of the flesh, but those who are according to the Spirit, the things of the Spirit. For the mind set on the flesh is death, but the mind set on the Spirit is life and peace, because the mind set on the flesh is hostile toward God; for it does not subject itself to the law of God, for it is not even able to do so, and those who are in the flesh cannot please God."*
> Romans 8:5-8

In order to make use of the law of the Spirit of life in Christ Jesus, Paul tells us we need to have a renewed mind, set on the Spirit. I will address this concept in much greater detail later, but you need to be aware of it now.

Keep in mind; I am not talking about someone's eternal destination. Once physical death removes the occupant from their body, they come under an entirely different set of spiritual laws. The presence of God's life in them brings their soul safely into the presence of the Lord. The bible tells us if a person accepts the sacrifice of Jesus for their sin, they will be saved; for "whoever will call upon the name of the Lord will be saved." (Romans 10:13) If they have life from God, that life is "Zoe" life, or eternal in nature. Since they have been living on this earth in the presence of God, death does not separate them from God—death only separates them from their body. If someone is separated from their body while they are still separated from God—in other words, not a Christian—then Satan owns them. They have no spiritual life in them and they remain separated from God. They go to Sheol—the bible calls it a place of torments—to await the resurrection for judgment. However, what I am addressing here is only the laws Christians function under while on this earth. I am using this as an argument to support the fact that the universe functions under legal principles. While one law can counteract another, the original still exists.

Disregard for law is called rebellion and is rooted in pride. It was pride that caused Satan to step out of God's law and attempt to establish his own law or basis for law. However, since the fear of God is the beginning of wisdom, Satan's law of the universe makes no sense, has no wisdom, and is destructive in nature. His law is based on lies and murder while God's law is based on truth and life. God's law liberates while Satan's law incarcerates. God's law brings freedom but Satan's brings addiction. Since our God is legal in nature, (legal in the sense that He has bound himself by a consistent, unchanging behavior standard), there are still rights available to Satan through God and God's laws. For instance, I believe God could not simply come down, destroy Satan, and kick him off the planet, because it would transgress God's own laws. Justice would have to prevail through truth and honor. There is a point in time when this action becomes viable, and it is in fact what Christ does when He returns the second time. The bible gives no statement about the reason this time is set, but it has been set. God also states He shortens those days for the sake of the elect. Again, we have no reference for the legal precedent which allows for this time. I presume it has to do with the last possible salvation of man.

Since God is a lawful God, (I know how superfluous that sounds, but indulge me), He is bound by His own law. There are spiritual laws in place involving ownership, authority and administration of the spiritual realms. They are not all defined in the bible and most can only be seen by looking at the biblical account of things that happened in the spiritual realms. We can also attempt to transpose God's nature as demonstrated on earth to the heavenly realms. In other words, the best we can really do is to make educated guesses. While we have been given absolute delineation of the spiritual laws as they apply to us, (they are defined in God's word), we can only surmise about the rest of the laws in effect for the spiritual realm.

For example, there was a legal exchange recorded about Moses' body. This dispute is referenced in the book of Jude. Satan claimed his title rights to the body of Moses, though no reason was given in Jude as to what legal claim he was exercising. I believe it was based on the same spiritual laws of sin and death that causes every human to be born into captivity. Adam's absolute failure in regards to the conditions of ownership for the earth gave Satan huge legal power over what takes place here. "But Michael the archangel, when he disputed with the devil and argued about the body of Moses, did not dare pronounce against him a railing judgment, but said, 'The Lord rebuke you!'" (Jude vs. 9).

Satan obviously had some difficulty in this particular court appearance with Michael presiding as legal counsel for the court. While we are not made privy to the legal arguments put forth in reference to this dispute, we know its outcome. In Matthew 17 we find three of the disciples, James, John, and Peter, on the mountain with Jesus when Moses and Elijah show up. No apparition but an 'in fact' appearance. (You will remember Elijah was taken to heaven in a fiery chariot, sidestepping death in the normal sense. He retained his body.) While there is no doubt Satan lost his legal argument for the body of Moses, we are not told what precedent was argued to allow this. It will be interesting to look at the transcripts of that trial when I get to heaven.

We get a little more insight into the legal aspects of the universe in the exchange recorded between God and Satan in reference to Job. Satan presented his case before the court and won some concessions from God the Father. Why did God allow this? Again we are not given a clear legal reference and can only make assumptions about the rationale. We do however get insight into the restrictive nature of Satan's legal claim on those who belong to God. He is not able to function outside of the authority of God himself, and gets permission for the things he does. Satan of course, uses this account to his advantage, relating it to bible believing Christians as proof that God won't protect them from harm. However, the account clearly demonstrates the benevolent delivering nature of our God if you read the last couple chapters of the book of Job. This account of Satan's interaction with God also shows how little power Satan has apart from what God allows him. It is further proof that his ownership of earth is provided by God's own legal structure (laws). There is obvious legal evidence of an unrepentant man's separation from God. He is a slave to the one he serves: the prince of darkness. However, those who belong to God are able to function outside these limitations. We will look at that in much greater definition in chapters five and six.

Does the earth really belong to Satan? What precedent proves this? Let's look at the recorded exchange between Satan and the Son of God recorded in Matthew:

"Again, the devil took Him to a very high mountain and showed Him all the kingdoms of the world and their glory; and he said to Him, 'All these things I will give You, if You fall down and worship me.' Then Jesus said to him, 'Go, Satan! For it is written, "you shall worship the Lord your God and serve Him only"' Then the devil left Him; and behold, angels came and began to minister to Him."
Matthew 4:8-11

Chapter 4

There is no objection from Jesus saying the kingdoms of this world weren't Satan's to give. He did not discount the authenticity of Satan's ownership. Jesus seemingly accepts this as fact and goes to the root of the argument. His rebuttal was based on a higher law: He was not free to worship whoever wanted to be worshipped, no matter how much the proponent owned and was able to offer. I believe this account clearly establishes Satan's legal claim to the kingdoms of this world. But wait—there's more!

Jesus called Satan a name that also acknowledges his reign.

"I will not speak with you much longer, for the prince of this world is coming. He has no hold on me, but the world must learn that I love the Father and that I do exactly what my Father has commanded me."
John 14:30-31 (NIV)

Jesus again acknowledges Satan's rule of the earth and its nations. However, Satan could lay no claim to Jesus. In all of His temptations and trials, He did not sin. We find sin to be the obstacle that defeats liberty. Romans 6:16 says, "Do you not know that when you present yourselves to someone as slaves for obedience, you are slaves of the one whom you obey, either of sin resulting in death, or of obedience resulting in righteousness?"

This is a very revealing scripture. It says we fall under the authority of those we obey. Jesus never obeyed Satan or His flesh and declared He only did those things the Father told Him to do. He could safely make the claim, "he has no hold on me". It takes little mental prowess to transpose this onto your own life. If you obey God, you belong to God. When you obey the sinful nature you belong to Satan. The difference for those who have the spirit of God within them is they can repent at any time, receive forgiveness and be cleansed by the blood of Jesus. In doing so, they are again set free from the law of sin and death (I John 1:9). Because of this spiritual law, we who are Christ's can always enter boldly into the throne room of God and receive the grace we so desperately need. Even so, this presents a strong argument for righteous living.

Satan's defeat was further demonstrated by the release of the captives. When Jesus said, "It is finished" it was finished, and so was Satan's hold over all the captives who had committed themselves to God in their lifetime. The legal requirements of God's law had been fulfilled, and Satan was left with very little.

Before we can go to what would come to pass, let me describe what existed up to that point. Jesus gave a parable showing what happened to the dead prior to His death:

"Now there was a rich man, and he habitually dressed in purple and fine linen, joyously living in splendor every day. And a poor man named Lazarus was laid at his gate, covered with sores, and longing to be fed with the crumbs which were falling from the rich man's table; besides, even the dogs were coming and licking his sores. Now the poor man died and was carried away by the angels to Abraham's bosom; and the rich man also died and was buried. In Hades he lifted up his eyes, being in torment, and saw Abraham far away and Lazarus in his bosom." "And he cried out and said, 'Father Abraham, have mercy on me, and send Lazarus so that he may dip the tip of his finger in water and cool off my tongue, for I am in agony in this flame.' But Abraham said, 'Child, remember that during your life you received your good things, and likewise Lazarus bad things; but now he is being comforted here, and you are in agony. And besides all this, between us and you there is a great chasm fixed, so that those who wish to come over from here to you will not be able, and that none may cross over from there to us.'" "And he said, 'Then I beg you, father, that you send him to my father's house—for I have five brothers—in order that he may

Chapter 4

warn them, so that they will not also come to this place of torment.' But Abraham said, 'They have Moses and the Prophets; let them hear them.' But he said, 'No, father Abraham, but if someone goes to them from the dead, they will repent!' But he said to him, 'If they do not listen to Moses and the Prophets, they will not be persuaded even if someone rises from the dead.'"
Luke 16:19-31

This parable establishes a number of things verified elsewhere. Those who died looking for God's promise went to a place of captivity but also to a place where they would be comforted. Jesus was not specific about the reason Lazarus was in "Abraham's bosom," as it was referred to, but history fills in the blanks a little bit. We know those who died looking for the promise were to be set free from captivity at the fulfillment of the promise. When the receipt for payment of the sin of those in captivity was presented, they would be released. Therefore, special conditions were made for those who awaited the promise. The sign of the acceptance of the promise was circumcision. By this simple act, they acknowledged their citizenship in the kingdom of Israel. This promise would also extend to the Gentile who would enter in through circumcision. The result would be, while they were indeed captive and apart from God in the sense of being in Sheol, they would not suffer the torment which was there for those who lived their lives for themselves.

There are many references to this in the bible. A number of terms relate to it. It is called Hades, lower parts of the earth, heart of the earth, the grave, Sheol and many other names. The children of Israel all knew they would go to Hades at their death. They knew Sheol would hold them and only by the power of God could they escape. However, there are also many references indicating they expected to be comforted there.

I hope this corrects some misconceptions that might exist at this point. Until Christ paid the price, the dead did not go to heaven. There were a few notable exceptions to this; Enoch, Moses, and Elijah were recorded as going to heaven. Beyond that, those waiting for a redeemer related to their death as going to Sheol. David said he hoped in the Lord to redeem his soul from Sheol (Psalm 49:15). Many others related to their death in the same terms.

When Jesus died and was buried, He accomplished much during those three days prior to His resurrection. Satan had nothing on Him and could not hold Him. He presented His blood on the mercy seat as proof of the paid price, and with the authority He received, He descended and set the captives free.

"But when Christ appeared as a high priest of the good things to come, He entered through the greater and more perfect tabernacle, not made with hands, that is to say, not of this creation; and not through the blood of goats and calves, but through His own blood, He entered the holy place once for all, having obtained eternal redemption."
Hebrews 9:11-12

Therefore it says, "When he ascended on high he led captive a host of captives, and he gave gifts to men." (Now this expression, "He ascended," what does it mean except that He also had descended into the lower parts of the earth?) "He who descended is Himself also He who ascended far above all the heavens, so that He might fill all things."
Ephesians 4:8-10

"For just as Jonah was three days and three nights in the belly of the sea monster, so will the Son of Man be three days and three nights in the heart of the earth."
Matthew 12:40-41

Chapter 4

"Remember these things, O Jacob, And Israel, for you are My servant; I have formed you, you are My servant, O Israel, you will not be forgotten by Me. 'I have wiped out your transgressions like a thick cloud And your sins like a heavy mist. Return to Me, for I have redeemed you.' Shout for joy, O heavens, for the LORD has done it! Shout joyfully, you lower parts of the earth; Break forth into a shout of joy, you mountains, O forest, and every tree in it; For the LORD has redeemed Jacob and in Israel He shows forth His glory. Thus says the LORD, your Redeemer, and the one who formed you from the womb..."
Isaiah 44:21-24

Satan is defeated, but still at liberty. As kingdom Christians you will deal with him many times and in many confrontations. Often we will present ourselves to unrighteousness and when we do, Romans 6 tells us we become its slave. Then, we need to do what John prescribes. "If we confess our sins, He is faithful and righteous to forgive us our sins and to cleanse us from all unrighteousness." (1 John 1:9) We have instant deliverance from our own fallibility if we are humble enough to turn to God and rely on it. Once we pass through the parameters of this scripture, we move into the light and "the blood of Jesus cleanses us from all sin." We again fall under, "the law of the Spirit of life in Christ Jesus" and it "has set you free from the law of sin and of death." (Romans 8:1-2)

You really need to understand this point. Satan can only have the power over you that you are willing or confused enough to give him. If you are free, then you are free. Unless, of course, you can be convinced you're not. When I was a boy growing up on a farm, we used an electric fence consisting of one wire stretched some distance across posts to confine our pigs. Pigs have rather poor eyesight, so they were unable to see the wire which enclosed them, but they learned at certain places they would encounter a sharp pain, so they would avoid those places. When we would change their pasture by part of the fence and giving them greater liberty, you even chase them across the place where the fence once ... n their own minds, they were still confined and made no ... eir greater liberty. We often do the same thing. However, in our case we have our carnal beliefs and the enemy who whispers "you can't" when indeed you can.

Satan has been defeated! This truth is yours if you will own it! Claim it. Speak it! It has been given to those of the Kingdom of Light to enforce, for now on this earth, the victory that Jesus won. He will come again. He will establish His throne on this earth. But for now, you are His chosen instrument to enforce the kingdom on this earth. To enforce the power of freedom in your life and in the lives He sends you to. You will lay hands on the sick and they will recover! You will cast out demons in His name! It is the Father's good will that you would produce much fruit and your fruit will remain. Even the spirits are subject to you. Your freedom cost our Lord His life. He paid a terrible price. He did it so He could set you free. Will you walk in that freedom?

> "THE SPIRIT OF THE LORD IS UPON ME,
> BECAUSE HE ANOINTED ME TO PREACH
> THE GOSPEL TO THE POOR.
> HE HAS SENT ME TO PROCLAIM
> RELEASE TO THE CAPTIVES,
> AND RECOVERY OF SIGHT TO THE BLIND,
> TO SET FREE THOSE WHO ARE OPPRESSED,
> TO PROCLAIM THE FAVORABLE YEAR OF THE LORD."

"And He closed the book, gave it back to the attendant and sat down; and the eyes of all in the synagogue were fixed on Him. And He began to say to them, 'Today this Scripture has been fulfilled in your hearing.'"
Luke 4:18-21

Chapter 5
The Naturalization Process

"But you are a chosen race, a royal priesthood, a holy nation, a people for God's own possession, so that you may proclaim the excellencies of Him who has called you out of darkness into His marvelous light; for you once were not a people, but now you are the people of God; you had not received mercy, but now you have received mercy. Beloved, I urge you as aliens and strangers to abstain from fleshly lusts which wage war against the soul."
1 Peter 2:9-10

In this world there are many laws and procedures relating to citizenship. Each nation has established some guidelines as to who can call themselves citizens of that nation and fall under the protection of its laws. In order to live in a country you either need to have permission to stay for a time or else be or become a citizen. The processes for obtaining citizenship are similar from country to country, with each government establishing its own laws and procedures. There is one method for obtaining citizenship to a country which is universal. All who are born naturally to citizens within any country are considered citizens of that country. You gain your citizenship by birth. So is it with the two kingdoms on this earth.

You begin your life on earth being born into the kingdom of darkness. It is your kingdom nationality. You don't choose it any more than you choose your earthly nationality. It was chosen for you by Adam. All who are born into this world are born into sin and death. They belong to the kingdom of darkness and the Prince of Darkness is their ruler. This is an important fact to know, as understanding your need for a deliverer is tied to the understanding that you're born into slavery. Your citizenship to the kingdom of darkness is by natural birth and unless you change your citizenship, you will die in the slavery you are born into. So who will set you free? "Wretched man that I am! Who will set me free from the body of this death?" (Romans 7:24)

> *"For he has rescued us from the kingdom of darkness and transferred us into the Kingdom of his dear Son, who purchased our freedom and forgave our sins."*
> *Colossians 1:13-14 (NLT)*

We are deeply in need of a redeemer at birth—in need of a deliverer—in need of a new citizenship. However, the prince of this world is pretty good at keeping his captives ignorant. Unless someone can present to you the gospel of the kingdom while you are a citizen of the kingdom of darkness, you will remain in the darkness.

If I was the Prince of Darkness and had the goal of deceiving all of God's creation, this is how I would accomplish my goals:

I would do everything in my power to redefine what constituted family. I would establish children as far away from parental supervision as I could by making it imperative in the minds of the citizens that both parents stay occupied at jobs during the better part of their waking hours. Pure greed and economics would be sufficient to drive this for me, if I could develop a communication system which would present the citizens with as many tantalizing diversions as possible. To help this along a little, I would encourage the females of the kingdom to redefine what constituted progressive femininity. It would be tied to economic gain and removed as far as possible from motherhood. I would put influences in society that would make "stay at home moms" seem primitive in their thinking. I could also set societal norms that would make husbands who support their wife's decision to stay home come off chauvinistic.

Once this had been established and women began to join the work force in droves, it would be very difficult to back out of, because world economics would be driven by two incomes. This would drive up prices by increased demand, making it very difficult for a single-income family.

If I were Satan, I would attempt to remove the idea that parents are qualified to teach their own children, so those who are most close to children and naturally most protective would have the least impact. After all, if you aren't trained or don't have a degree, who are you to think you should teach? I would infiltrate the educational institutions with those who most closely embrace this type of thinking. If they began to think along moral and biblical lines, I would try as hard as I could to get them to fall—get them to discredit themselves by their own actions. I would resist them in any way I could. Any temptation to sin I could imagine I would throw in their path. On the other hand, I would make the way as smooth as possible for those who were secular in their thinking. This would of course go double for those institutions whose purpose was to develop teachers or journalists. Eventually those people who were considered thinkers wouldn't really be thinkers at all but only those who espoused all the ideas I wanted espoused. Since they would reinforce themselves by themselves, no one would realize it.

I would develop an educational system that rewarded secular thinking. I would also try to remove any vestiges of the living God from the curriculum. I would introduce the concepts of pluralism and universalism as truth. This would discourage a "one way is right" idea and promote divergent thinking. I would manipulate the concept of multiculturalism to make people who believe Christ is the Messiah look intolerant. This would be done in such a way as to make those who tried to interfere appear stupid and narrow minded, since I would have already woven the idea of acceptance of divergent thinking into the universalistic theme. (Being narrow minded is encouraged in the Bible by the way, i.e. straight is the way and narrow the path that leads to life). Of course, Christianity would not be part of acceptable thinking.

As much as possible, I would remove the teaching of truth from educational institutions. This could be done by substituting biblical truth with a lie and calling it science. I would introduce a theory of evolution as a science. If I was really good, I could accomplish this even though it didn't even meet established physical and biological laws of science or the parameters set forth in science to define a valid theory. I would make certain institutions of learning were filled with those who embraced evolution and accepted this non-science as science. If it removed the need to be responsible to a creator, people would embrace it well enough. I would also reinforce this with this next idea:

I would cause man to worship science as the savior he needed. I would make certain that scientists would hold titles which men would learn to respect. Letters! That's what I would need! I would give them letters after their name so people would respect them. Pretty soon it would require letters for people to believe you knew anything or were really able to think at all. This plan is showing promise!

Now here's an idea: I could convince the Christian clergy they weren't really qualified to counsel people, and convince the citizens of this world their only hope was a secular psychologist so they would not go to biblical counseling at all. Since psychology wouldn't have the ability to deliver people from their sin, it would soon start to excuse the sin as normal, i.e. Homosexuality, sexual promiscuity, rebelling against Godly authority, etc. Also, I could use greed on the part of secular psychologists to encourage the over-diagnosis of mental disorders such as Bipolar disorder, ADD, depression and so on. These are all labels which accurately define human behavior patterns, but when used by a secular thinker, can imprison people since they present no hope of freedom apart from drugs. As the Prince of this world, once I had accomplished getting them accepted as defined patterns which excused behavior, I would have a pit which could trap anyone willing to fall into it. It could be given the title of science to make it even more acceptable.

I would prosper those in the media whose thinking was secular. There would be no obstacles I would put in their path. The more they discounted the Bible, the more I would leave them alone and the more success I would try to give them. As more and more carnal thinkers moved into positions of authority within the news organizations, the less I would have to attend to, because the natural system would be self-propagating. As the media began to parade the lies as truth, I could deceive more and more people into thinking they were being enlightened by the lies I wanted established. Of course I would have already developed systems of awards which would be given to those who most closely followed my thinking, so people would receive their lies more readily since they held such respected awards. Thus, I would establish a lie as the truth and establish the truth as a lie.

Mankind's natural propensity to fall into pride would make this whole process easier. Since mankind is born into sin, all are born with a tendency to exalt themselves above others. I would appeal to the pride of man. I would introduce concepts of life that would define success by standards which have little relevance to true value. Success in the world would be defined by economic standards and not by moral standards. I would cause moral standards to be limited by situational ethics as much as possible.

Chapter 5

I know men who are considered very successful in this world who are abject failures in the reality of the truth of the universe. Deep inside, they know it, but the world reinforces their captivity and they never even go looking for the liberty meant for mankind. They shake off the apprehension and pat themselves on the back for their ability to meet this world's standards. If I could sell this lie well enough, it would entrap millions. I would make certain that citizens in the kingdom of darkness define themselves by what they can accomplish and to take pride in the amassing of wealth.

I would make comfort and security good goals, and convince those who are part of this world to define theirs and other's success by how well they can obtain those two things. Of course I would define security as not being in want of daily needs over time. In other words, it is not enough to have the needs of that day, but if you can lay ahead for days yet to come, you have greater security. The more you could lay up the more secure and thus the more successful. Can you see the pride in that? James said we don't even know if we have tomorrow. How stupid to define success by how many tomorrows we've laid up for. Let me clarify so you don't build a case out of what I am not saying. I am not saying it is stupid to save or lay up for later years. I am saying it is stupid to define success and worth by how many future days you've laid up for or by how much wealth you've amassed. It is prudent to prepare for famine but not wise to believe you are what you've stored up or to put your hope in it. It is prudent to work hard but not wise to glory in what abilities God has given you, since you did not create them in yourself. However, as the Prince of Darkness, I would make certain clear thinking was discouraged and made outright ridiculous whenever possible.

I would make certain those who had the least value would receive the greatest economic enhancement and those who had the most value received little. Those who entertained us would be the highest on the food chain, because I would already have established entertainment as one of the great comforts the citizens need. I would get science to develop more and more comfort enhancements so that society would be full of self absorbed consumers. I would pay those who lead us toward God little so people would relate to them as really not worth paying at all. This would discourage any who might think of pursuing God for financial gain from heading in that direction and so stumble upon the truth by accident. This would also give the deceived the wrong heroes to follow.

Do you see how essential it was for the prince of this world to get the social fabric to break free from the concept of a creator? If people were created with certain gifts and graces, how then could they take pride in them? But if you were just a little further down the evolutionary chain, now that was something you could feel good about! That could be defined as successful! Eugenics was born from this strain of pride and much of the rush to genetic engineering has its roots in this sin. However, if a creator is not involved, why not? Someone has to determine the future, why not those who are the most intelligent? Equipped with these types of lies, a skewed matrix of deception can be woven into the fabric of the thinking of its captives and voila! The world gets further and further from the truth all the while believing it is defining truth. The ruler of this world is so very subtle and how deceived its inhabitants.

Those are the things I would do as the prince of this world to lead its citizens away from a living God and into destruction. It doesn't take too much intelligence really to come up with these ideas. It's not really rocket science. This strategy is already being displayed in our culture. The evidence of this thinking is being played out in the world as we watch. The people being used aren't aware of their role as pawns in the hand of the ruler of this world. To many of them, it is simply enlightened thinking. They have come upon it by revelation, and without the light being shed in their understanding by the kingdom of Light, to them it seems supremely more intelligent than real truth.

Chapter 5

The coup de grace would be to try to pull the wool over my archenemy—the church. Try to make the concepts of a spiritual kingdom seem very unreal and farfetched. Convince the clergy that big programs and fortressed churches were pretty spiritual and anything even remotely spooky should be avoided at all costs. Establish, if I was able, the lie that all spiritual power is no longer relevant. It was only given for centuries past. I would try to get the message of the kingdom as far away as possible from the minds of those who were supposed to be its citizens. I could establish an idea Christianity was not supposed to be part of a daily life and have it relegated to Sunday as much as possible. The truths I would establish in my kingdom would be so divergent from truth and so established as reality, that any thought of a supernatural kingdom functioning on the face of the earth would seem extremely farfetched, even for a believer. All of this would make the church pretty impotent to accomplish its real goals.

The problem for those Jesus has set free and made citizens of the kingdom of Light is that the brainwashing for the citizens of the kingdom of darkness begins early and is reinforced throughout the early years of a child's life. The greater the wealth of a nation, the greater the level of brainwashing and the more difficult it is to change their citizenship and adopt the social customs of a different kingdom. The more time a child spends away from any parent or godly influence, the more their thinking becomes distorted. The more time they spend under the influence of distorted media, the more diluted their understanding of the truth. Music, television, and the movie industry are all well used by the prince of this world to establish his lie. The public educational system is by and large governed by secular ideas as well as most universities. All of these things work to keep you firmly within the mindset of the kingdom of darkness.

One day you're walking along as a citizen of the kingdom of darkness and the truth is revealed to you. It must be supernaturally revealed to you because you are not able to come upon it on your own. Possibly someone being obedient to the role of a believer presents to you the message of salvation—or if you're lucky, the gospel of the kingdom—and you are lead by the Spirit into the truth of Jesus. It's not even by your own intelligence, but by the intervention of the Lord by His Spirit.

"No one can come to Me unless the Father who sent Me draws him; and I will raise him up on the last day."
John 6:44

Jesus said to him, "I am the way, and the truth, and the life; no one comes to the Father but through Me."
John 14:6

Since God is not willing that any should perish (II Peter 3:9) He will give all a chance to be saved and calls each one in His own way. So one day, the Father calls and you hear and respond to that call positively. You look toward God and His principles and you determine to accept them as your own. You see the need you have for a redeemer and you see your absolute moral and spiritual poverty apart from such a redeemer, and you call on His name. It says, "All who call upon the name of the Lord will be saved". (Romans 10:13) As you repent of being lord of your own life and turn toward the life which is being held out, you are born again. Your "born again" birth is a citizenship by birth to an entirely different kingdom—the kingdom of God. "Jesus answered and said to him, 'Truly, truly, I say to you, unless one is born again he cannot see the kingdom of God.'" (John 3:3) You become 'born again' through your prayer and your change of heart and your confession of faith, and suddenly a whole new kingdom and life is opened up to you which has never been seen by you before.

What you "see" is spiritual—supernatural—and entirely foreign in its concept. You see it by revelation in your soul and it is completely unlike anything you have ever seen before. It functions under a different set of principles and having come from the established lies of the kingdom of darkness, its truths seem surreal to you. You hold eagerly to the idea of life in eternity with the Lord and try to comprehend the rest of what you are seeing. Many times, if a new believer doesn't surround himself with those who know the truth, it becomes very easy to fall back into the captivity of the lies of the enemy and attempt to live out the Christian experience by adhering to the rules and laws of this world. This is deadly to a kingdom experience and pretty well neutralizes a believer from the power which could be theirs.

I have noticed God really nurtures the brand new believer and extends grace after grace. The presence of evidence of a supernatural force working on behalf of the new believer is readily discernable at the beginning. Later, however, we are expected to grow up and walk by faith, so there is less and less physical evidence and more and more spiritual revelation. We begin to truly "walk by faith and not by sight" (2 Corinthian 5:7). About faith I must say this: one cannot live by worldly principles and experience a faith walk. This is the reason for this book. You must learn the nature of the kingdom Jesus has birthed you into and begin to put it on, or you will not be able to live a vibrant kingdom walk and you will not experience the victory which is expressed in Romans where we are told we are "more than conquerors". (Romans 8:37)

Having set the stage, may I help you understand how citizenship works? I am a citizen of the United States and as such, while living in the United States I am protected by its laws. If I live in Spain, though I may have the right to call on the embassy of the United States since I am a U.S. citizen, I still fall under the laws of Spain as long as I live there and I am not protected completely by the laws of my citizenship. If I choose to continue to live in that country, my citizenship in the US does me little good. However, since I am a citizen, I can at any time board an airplane and fly back to the country of my citizenship and once again enjoy whatever benefits my citizenship brings me. The one exception to this would be if I lived in another country as an ambassador. I would then have diplomatic immunity from the laws of the country where I lived and fall completely under the protection and laws of the United States. This provision has great kingdom application also, which we will look at in Chapter 7. For now, hold on to the fact your citizenship only guarantees you the right to all the benefits when you put yourself under the government which instituted that protection.

If you are somewhat intuitive, I am sure you are getting a glimmer of where this is going. While you are a citizen of the kingdom of darkness, you are subject to its laws, good or bad. When you change your citizenship, you fall under the laws of your new kingdom as long as you change your residence to or live in the new kingdom to which you have been expatriated. If you continue walking in the kingdom where you once held your citizenship, you will not enjoy all of the benefits of your new citizenship. You will fall under the local laws of the kingdom where you reside and the advantages of changing your citizenship will not be realized. As a matter of fact, you will experience from those with whom you live a certain local resentment to the fact you abandoned your old citizenship, unless you can keep your new loyalties a secret. Thus many Christians receive their citizenship into the kingdom of Light only to continue living in the kingdom of darkness and never realizing the benefits of their new kingdom. Also many times, since they wish to remain viable in their old relationships and manner of living, they refrain from disclosing much about who they have become.

So, how do you relocate? First, remember we are speaking of two kingdoms. Though they are both located on earth, they function in accordance with different principles. When you are a citizen of the kingdom of this world, you find pleasure in the natural physical world. These pleasures draw your attention. You take pleasure in things you can embrace with the senses—hearing, touching, tasting, smelling, and seeing. The need to find favorable experiences within these areas drives you. Even relationships are defined by how well these needs are met. You pretty much set your mind on pleasure and its sources. You pursue them, enjoy them, and gain your sense of well being from them. When you get saved, you still find pleasure in tangible things. Beautiful scenery is still pleasant to the eyes. The sweet smell of a lilac bush still elicits pleasure, as does the taste and smell of a nicely cooked steak. Silk still feels rich, and music played well still touches your soul. This raises a daunting question—is God asking you to do the impossible? Since you still experience all these things, and continue to live and work amongst people who pursue such things, how in the world can you fully relocate? Fear not, there is hope in chapter six.

> *"And you were dead in your trespasses and sins, in which you formerly walked according to the course of this world, according to the prince of the power of the air, of the spirit that is now working in the sons of disobedience. Among them we too all formerly lived in the lusts of our flesh, indulging the desires of the flesh and of the mind, and were by nature children of wrath, even as the rest."*
> *Ephesians 2:1-4*

Chapter 6
Entering the Kingdom of Light

We've asked, "How in the world do you relocate?" Well, the relocation to your new kingdom takes place in the 'mind' or, as it is also referred to, the heart. Proverbs 23:7 says, "For as a man thinks in his heart, so is he." (Amplified) It is your thinking which has to change. The way you always thought about life and values, that is, what is right and wrong, valuable and common, worthy or unworthy, must undergo a complete transformation. Your sight must be changed so you view the world through a different lens. What you watch and listen to will need to be determined by your new value system. You will become less concerned about what you will eat, what you will drink, or what you should put on. You will need to be completely reprogrammed. All of the brainwashing the kingdom of darkness has put into you will need to be removed.

This does not happen passively. You will need to focus on this transformation to make it happen.

> *"And do not be conformed to this world, but be transformed by the renewing of your mind, so that you may prove what the will of God is, that which is good and acceptable and perfect."*
> Romans 12:2

> *"We are destroying speculations and every lofty thing raised up against the knowledge of God, and we are taking every thought captive to the obedience of Christ."*
> 2 Corinthians 10:5

Notice the very active verbs used in these scriptures: "transformed"; "renewing"; "destroying"; "taking"; this is not a peaceful process and requires purposeful effort. Up to this point, all of your thoughts have been validated by the world from which you came. You have been programmed to think about life in a certain

Chapter 6

way. Define success in a certain way. Establish goals and arrange life around a worldly perspective. When you get saved, your mind is in serious need of renewal. You need to know this responsibility becomes yours, so you might become actively engaged in it. Until this process has been accomplished your thinking will remain hopelessly hostile to God.

> *"For those who are according to the flesh set their minds on the things of the flesh, but those who are according to the Spirit, the things of the Spirit. For the mind set on the flesh is death, but the mind set on the Spirit is life and peace, because the mind set on the flesh is hostile toward God; for it does not subject itself to the law of God, for it is not even able to do so, and those who are in the flesh cannot please God."*
> Romans 8:5-8

Do not gloss over the magnitude of change this passage necessitates. It reveals some very great kingdom truths. If you continue to think in the same way as you have always thought, you will be unable to please God. I have watched this pattern in Christians for many years. This is how I have seen it happen in many new believers: Let's take a fictitious believer called Jim. As he gains citizenship into the kingdom of God, Jim might change a few of his outward habits. He might stop smoking—or drinking—or using foul language. Simply by association with fellow believers, Jim picks up some improved mannerisms. Old friends might even mention how different Jim has become and stop calling. Externally, Jim appears a bit different. However, there is no real transformation of his life.

After a length of time in this mode, lethargy and apathy set in. Things aren't really much different. Oh sure, he can't sin as much, but what satisfaction is there in that? One Sunday morning Jim wakes up, looks at the clock and realizes the next four hours will have little excitement. Announcements will be at this time, the choir will sing at that time, offering taken at this time. The pastor will get up and speak for x minutes on y topic and probably do a pretty good job. If the service is really inspirational, it might even leave the congregation with some warm fuzzies for a bit. Perhaps, if it is a charismatic church, there might be some evidence of the gifts which will create some diversion. Maybe dancing and flag waving can be introduced, making it even more entertaining. The service will close with a song. People will get up and mill around and tell each other how good the worship was. Then everyone will get into their cars and drive back to their homes. If Jim is really committed he might repeat this process on Wednesday night, and sometimes even on a Sunday night as well.

Other than giving up free time, little else has changed for many believers. Monday through Friday they will fill the workplace and the commuter lanes and go to and fro. They will watch TV when they get home, help the kids with their homework—or not—go to bed, get up the next day and repeat the process all over again. When the next service comes that whole scenario called "church" will take place just like before, complete with choir and preaching and doughnuts.

I am going to interrupt here and make a request. Please, absolutely do not decide this is so descriptive of what your Christian experience is like that it is pointless to keep on doing this 'church thing' any longer. I have watched some people do this. They stop doing what they were doing which was right because they were doing it the wrong way. If this scenario describes your Christian experience, don't disregard what you've been doing right, but with a wrong understanding. Continue to do what is right, but take the next step into maturity and do it with a transformed heart! Change your understanding not your good habits. Begin the dynamic process of renewing your mind! This requires your effort.

"But seek first His kingdom and His righteousness, and all these things will be added to you."
Matthew 6:31-32

Seek first! What in the world is Jesus talking about?! And again with the 'active' verbs! Isn't it all done for you by Jesus? How do you 'seek first'? Isn't that what you're doing when you go to church? Not really.

The "seek first" passage truly defines what this book is about. What you used to spend hours planning and thinking about, now becomes passé. You used to worry about your job and your raise and your income and bank account. How can you pay rent? Make the house payment? How can you have enough to eat? How about if you get sick? How can you replace the family car which is starting to give you troubles? All of these things occupied most of your non entertainment thinking. They were such a concern to you that you would spend money on things which would get your mind off them.

> *"So this I say, and affirm together with the Lord, that you walk no longer just as the Gentiles also walk, in the futility of their mind, being darkened in their understanding, excluded from the life of God because of the ignorance that is in them, because of the hardness of their heart."*
> Ephesians 4:17-19

This is the sadness of a kingdom of darkness life. It has no life in it. When unsaved, we are darkened in our understanding by the brainwashing of the prince of that kingdom. When we become a Christian, we need to quit walking in the futility of our thinking and begin a whole different way of walking.

> *"For we walk by faith, not by sight."*
> 2 Corinthians 5:7

Are you beginning to see the vast course change you are asked to make when becoming a citizen in the kingdom of God? I can assure you it is worth it. I can also assure you it won't happen unless you get involved in the process. I will discuss some tips on how to go about that, but right now, I am trying to give you an understanding of how complete that process needs to be. You must stop seeing life as the pursuit of comfort and security. Those are worthless goals which have no eternal impact. Worldly living is about momentary impact. Kingdom living is about eternal impact.

At this point, if this message is new to you, you are probably asking yourself, "Well that's fine, but what does that mean really? I still need to eat, drink, and be clothed. How does that happen unless I get involved in the process?"

That's a valid thought. Yes, you need to eat and drink and be clothed. Yes, you need to pay the rent. You will still need to get up and go to work. Jesus is not asking you to walk the streets waiting for your next hand out. So what will change? The change will be both vast and subtle. I understand the oxymoronic drift of that, but it is an accurate statement nonetheless.

First, the 'vast' part of the change. The Bible says this about your daily needs:

> *"Do not worry then, saying, 'What will we eat?' or 'What will we drink?' or 'What will we wear for clothing?' "For the Gentiles eagerly seek all these things; for your heavenly Father knows that you need all these things."*
> *Matthew 6:31-33*

At the start of my Christian experience, this passage seemed nice, but unworkable. I had great difficulty owning it, especially when I entered into some rather hard financial times right after I got saved. Only as I began to have an understanding of kingdom thinking did it make sense to me.

Chapter 6

God is not unaware of your needs. He is also not enthralled with comfort as a goal. He has promised you certain things. He will give you food and clothing, and with that help you learn to be content. Paul addresses this subject rather well in his letter to the Philippians;

> *"Not that I speak from want, for I have learned to be content in whatever circumstances I am. I know how to get along with humble means, and I also know how to live in prosperity; in any and every circumstance I have learned the secret of being filled and going hungry, both of having abundance and suffering need. I can do all things through Him who strengthens me."*
> *Philippians 4:11-13*

Most of us are afraid to trust God for our daily needs because we realize His thoughts about our daily needs are different than ours. We are afraid He might not keep us in the comfort to which we've grown accustomed. There is too much biblical evidence of people going through hardship for our tastes, and having grown up in a world which devotes itself to the pursuit of comfort, it became our objective as well. To totally abandon a perspective which idolizes pleasure and comfort is too austere for our tastes. One of the biggest problems we see with living by kingdom standards is we WON'T be able to pursue all of those things we used to pursue. They will have to remain secondary and the kingdom will have to become primary.

God is not opposed to blessing His children. He sometimes provides extravagantly for comfort and pleasure. I have had times when God provided such opulent comfort that I was almost embarrassed. Paul spoke not only about humble means but also about prosperous living. Sometimes I have had to learn the secret of being filled. (That one is a little easier to learn, I might add.) The Bible is full of servants of God who lived quite prosperously. However, you will need to trust God to give you good things and not seek to provide them for yourself. That's way too little control for most people—until they have their minds renewed.

The kingdom road is narrow—not wide like the road the world is on. There is much benefit to the kingdom road. Please don't delude yourself into thinking maybe you can have a little of both kingdoms in your life. You will love the one and hate the other, or you will hate the one and love the other. The wide road and the narrow road are in opposition to one another. They travel in opposite directions. There is no way to have a little of both. No real middle ground exists.

Here is the subtlety of the change I talked about:

If you become a kingdom minded Christian, you will look like everyone else who is living life but you will be completely different! You will go to work. You will probably own a car. You will live with your mate and your children. You will receive promotions, buy a house with a mortgage, and buy groceries at the local grocery store. If you live in the United States you will shop at Wal-Mart, Penny's, Target, etc, have a retirement plan, get health insurance, go to the movies (of course not too often because you will be discriminating in what you watch), go to the beach if it is handy, take vacations, have pets, laugh, cry and live life. To anyone who casually observes you, you will seem just like everyone else in society. That is the subtlety. You will be completely different on the inside.

So what will that difference be? Jesus showed us.

"I can do nothing on My own initiative. As I hear, I judge; and My judgment is just, because I do not seek My own will, but the will of Him who sent Me."
John 5:30

Chapter 6

The subtlety is the motivation behind what you do. Your job or business will not be about making money–though you will need to make money. You will live where you live not simply because you choose to–though you will chose to live somewhere. This is what is supposed to happen as you enter the kingdom. Your desires are to become secondary and His will is to become primary. This paradigm shift is essential if you wish to enter the kingdom of God. Your choices will no longer rest on you. You will do nothing on your own initiative, but you will only do what the Father wills. Where you work will not be a place to enhance your social status or gain wealth, but will become the field where God's kingdom is advanced. You will choose your job not on your desire for your self fulfillment but by what God has defined as His will for your life. Where you live will not be about the weather or the schools or the perks, but about where God wants you. Your desires will no longer determine your course. You will subject yourself to His wishes. Since you walk by faith and not by sight, a natural assessment of the chances for success will be secondary to the spiritual leading of the Father. You will do what you're told and not what your mind may say is the best course. Relationship to the Lord will be the necessary center to the things you do because your success going forward will rest on your ability to hear the voice of your King.

If this whole concept is making you nervous, let me add this. God has instilled in you the desires of your heart. If you have an intense desire to work with children, you can feel certain it is God who put it there. If you would like to work outdoors those desires are not there by happenstance. If you are drawn to and gifted in music, you did not come about this on your own. Whatever you long to do and be which is not about base values such as comfort or security, those "real' things which burn in your imagination, they were put there by God and it is God who will cause them to come to pass as you serve Him. Recall this passage in Ephesians which says;

> *"For we are His workmanship, created in Christ Jesus for good works, which God prepared beforehand so that we would walk in them."*
> *Ephesians 2:10*

He knew who you were when He created you. (Remember, part of your kingdom transformation is getting over the lie you are a biological evolutionary advancement from the ape.) The bible tells us we were designed by God who knew us since the foundation of the earth. He knew where He was going to have you be born, what your IQ would be, when in history you would live and made plans to use you for His purpose. He built your desires into you for His purposes, and will use those desires to help motivate you to be what He created you to be. He knows whether you will accept the truth of the kingdom message or not and if you are going to refuse the message of the kingdom; He has also already created your replacement who won't refuse to fill your function in the kingdom. You can choose to never enter the kingdom of heaven until you die, if you want. I urge you not to want that. You will feel a bit disappointed in eternity knowing how God would have used you.

When a person changes their citizenship from one country to the next, only a few countries will allow you to have dual citizenship. The kingdom of God is not one of these. However, if you have chosen to live your Christian life within the confines of the kingdom of darkness, you still have a citizenship in the kingdom of light. At any time, you may decide to relocate your thinking and enter into the benefits which can come from being a citizen which enters into the kingdom of God.

Chapter 6

As long as you continue living by worldly principles you cannot benefit from your new citizenship—you will not enter the kingdom of God. In this chapter I have addressed your responsibilities to change your citizenship to a citizen of the kingdom of God. In the remaining chapters I will address the awesome benefits which come from making yourself responsible to your new citizenship and entering the kingdom. While you give up your control over your course by being a kingdom Christian, what you gain is worth every instance of the control you give up.

> *"Do not be afraid, little flock, for your Father has chosen gladly to give you the kingdom. Sell your possessions and give to charity; make yourselves money belts which do not wear out, an unfailing treasure in heaven, where no thief comes near nor moth destroys. For where your treasure is, there your heart will be also."*
> Luke 12:32-34

Chapter 7
Your Mission, Should You Choose to Accept It

"Now all these things are from God, who reconciled us to Himself through Christ and gave us the ministry of reconciliation, namely, that God was in Christ reconciling the world to Himself, not counting their trespasses against them, and He has committed to us the word of reconciliation. Therefore, we are ambassadors for Christ, as though God were making an appeal through us; we beg you on behalf of Christ, be reconciled to God."
2 Corinthians 5:18-21

Imagine you are sitting at home and the phone rings. Someone picks it up and then hands it to you. With an incredulous look on their face, they say, "It's for you and it's the President." Unless you happen to be a high ranking official of some sort, I would imagine a number of questions would go through your mind as you reached for the phone. And reach for the phone you would, even if you voted for the opposite party in the last election. Chances are you wouldn't put the President on hold. You would listen intently as he said, "I would like to have you represent this country to another nation. I would like to appoint you to the post of the U.S. ambassador to Ghana."

Your immediate thoughts might be, "I'm not qualified!" Or "I can't do that!" I doubt you would think, "I have more important things to do. Maybe some other time. I have a camping trip planned, not to mention my golf tournament on Sunday." No, I think you would be astounded by the honor you had just been shown.

Imagine the President continues: "I have researched your background, know who you are and have determined you have the qualities I need for this position. I will give you time to equip yourself and I will provide you with the information you need. After sufficient time to prepare, I am sending you to Ghana to represent us. You will be afforded all the honor and power that goes with that office. Any support you need the United States government will provide for you. I personally will handle all of your requests and make certain you have what you need to prepare. You will represent our country to the nation where I am sending you and act as my personal representative. Your title and position will begin today and you will leave in six months. All the resources of this government will be at your disposal to accomplish this purpose."

Would you tell the President "No"? I think not. You would need time to adjust to the idea, but in the end, you would feel rather honored. As you adjusted to your new title, you would begin to prepare for the adventure that lay ahead of you, collecting all the information you could on the position itself and what was required. If the President offered some briefings and classes, you would be eager to attend. If he told you that he was available to you on a regular basis, you would indeed spend some time talking to him.

Six months later, well-read and prepared by hours of study, you are called in by the President for one final briefing. You have come to know him quite well and you chat comfortably as he and his advisors brief you on the current situation that exists where you were going. The President informs you that Ghana has acknowledged your accreditation and you are cleared to represent the United States as his diplomat. Equipped with an understanding of the relationship between your country and the one you will be going to, you eagerly take your family and board a jet bound for the country of the President's choosing. You would probably be feeling apprehension, excitement and a little awe.

There are many interesting similarities between the role of an international ambassador and our role as ambassadors for the kingdom of God. However, it is very possible that as you read Paul's passage in Corinthians addressing ambassadorship, you might not be very aware of that office or understand the position as it exists in the world. The office has been recognized throughout the world throughout time. Did you know that the ambassador is the highest position held by any outside official in the receiving country? Within the receiving country there is no one from the sending country who carries greater authority other than the one who appointed and accredited the ambassador. (In our scenario, the President.)

The Vienna Convention of Diplomatic Relations of 1961 opens with this statement: "Recalling that peoples of all nations from ancient times have recognized the status of diplomatic agents." It continues to define all that is entailed. The rights and privileges as well as the responsibilities that frame the role of ambassador have been accepted and understood over the centuries. However, we seldom spend much time thinking about those unless we are part of that diplomatic community. If you have accepted Christ as your Lord and Savior and are entering into the kingdom of heaven, you now are part of the diplomatic community. Your assignment, should you wish to accept it, is to be an ambassador for the kingdom of God. When I read the parameters and definitions the Vienna convention afforded to diplomats and saw the similarities to what the word of God had to say, I realized that the calling we have been given is awesome. The comparison made by Paul and Peter to our role as ambassadors takes on even greater meaning as one looks at what being an ambassador involves.

The appointed ambassador to a nation is afforded the highest honors given to dignitaries by both the receiving country and the sending country. Only heads-of-state are given higher status. Ambassadors are considered plenipotentiary, meaning possessing full powers to represent the head-of-state for the country for which he or she is appointed

I would like to make some comparisons as to how international law regards the office of an ambassador and how this relates to you as an appointed ambassador of the kingdom of God. When reading the passage in 2nd Corinthians it may seem Paul speaks rather casually of this position. Since the Bible tells us he was educated in the best schools of his day and history says that ambassadors have been defined similarly throughout history, I know he was not ignorant of the scope of his assertion. Unless otherwise indicated, all secular references I quote are from the Vienna Convention of Diplomatic Relations of 1961. This international agreement did not redefine the office, but simply listed the parameters accepted by the International community as accepted practice through the centuries. The similarities to your kingdom ambassadorship are noted below.

Here are some of the statements within the articles for the Vienna Conference I find most interesting in comparison to what God says about our role. I will let you connect the dots as you read. The similarities are quite apparent.

Article 3

1. The functions of a diplomatic mission consist, inter alia, in:

(a) Representing the sending State in the receiving State;

You are appointed to represent the kingdom of God in the kingdom of this world. You are a resident ambassador. That is, you live within the borders of the receiving kingdom. Your role as biblically defined is "so that you may proclaim the excellencies of Him who has called you"

(b) Protecting in the receiving State the interests of the sending State and of its nationals, within the limits permitted by international law;

In other words, you are there to advance the interests of the kingdom you represent, creating support for the kingdom of heaven and its inhabitants. You are free to do this within the limits set by God's universal spiritual law.

(c) Negotiating with the Government of the receiving State;

You will be the contact point for the highest government official of the receiving state. Here in this kingdom, you will address the head-of-state directly if you need. The head-of-state for the kingdom of darkness is Satan. I like an anecdote told about Smith Wigglesworth, a British pastor known for his healing ministry around the turn of the 20th century. He awoke one night to see a figure standing at the foot of his bed. He recognized that it was Satan himself, and when he determined who it was, he simply said. "Oh. It's just you." He then turned over and went back to sleep. You see, there is no real need to be all awestruck. You actually have greater authority in Jesus name, since Satan's kingdom is currently an occupied territory that was conquered almost two thousand years ago.

(d) Ascertaining by all lawful means conditions and developments in the receiving State, and reporting thereon to the Government of the sending State;

As an ambassador, you are expected to represent the interests of the receiving country through diplomatic channels to your kingdom, bringing requests for aid and help for the country you serve in to the head-of-state of your country. You are to be a benefit to the receiving kingdom. As a matter of fact, part of the power an ambassador has within the kingdom he stationed in is his ability to benefit that nation and make things happen. In the kingdom of God your diplomatic correspondence is accomplished through prayer.

(e) Promoting friendly relations between the sending State and the receiving State, and developing their economic, cultural and scientific relations.

In our application, you don't become like Ghana's population in practice and activity. You are in this kingdom—not of this kingdom. You maintain your relational circle of influence so that you can promote the goals of your kingdom, but not by entering into the same activities that your government might deem inappropriate. To illustrate, an ambassador from the U.S. will not express approval to a country which demonstrates disregard for their population's civil rights.

Article 22

1. The premises of the mission shall be inviolable. The agents of the receiving State may not enter them, except with the consent of the head of the mission.

A "mission" is the offices and dwellings officially used by the ambassador, meaning embassies in the contemporary context. I believe, wherever you are placed by God falls under the same provisions as indicated by Article 22, whether it is home, office or church. This means Satan has no authority to enter into your home, office or church unless you give him that authority. Before I understood this, my home came under rather intense spiritual attack. Everyone in the house began experiencing bad dreams each night, the house was full of fear with no reason attached, and my family began to get sick. I sought God about it and He told me that what was happening in my home was spiritual in nature. I was to take the authority I had been given in the name of Christ and "clean house", so to speak. I did and peace returned. A while later we came under a similar attack. Knowing what it was and what to do, I again demanded that the property where we dwelt be considered inviolable by the kingdom of darkness. I declared it an embassy for the kingdom of God in the name of Jesus Christ. Peace returned once more.

I asked the Lord why I was required to make this statement more than once. His answer surprised me but made sense. He said that every time I yield ground to the enemy and give in to sin, I am inviting Satan to be my master, putting the mission under his authority. Whenever that happened, I would need to repent and again assert the authority that I desired there—which of course was God. Now if our home is accosted by such attacks, I know to seek God and determine where it is I have allowed Satan a foothold and repent, restoring the sovereignty of God to my home or office.

A little aside here if I might. The kingdom of God is not a place of lawlessness. It is a place where law and authority work as they were intended, and anyone who does not accept the structure ordained by God has no chance of entering the kingdom. I have heard some Christians suggest throwing out all established order and starting over. Flaws in the structure are never reason to throw out the structure. They are reasons to remodel, not to remove the foundation. It is His will for the authority structure to exist. God has established order and authority in His kingdom. If you are unable to submit to the authority that God has ordained, you will exist outside of the kingdom, for in the kingdom, God's will is done. If there are those to whom He has given authority in His kingdom who abuse it, trust me, He will deal with them in due season. It may not be as quickly as our impatient, fast food mentalities demand, but He will put things back in order. If you believe that where you are currently attending church is not of God, then seek God for His direction about where He wants you to be. I guarantee it will be within a biblical structure somewhere. Mostly though, He expects you to let your light shine where He planted you. Here in the U.S. our ranks are filled with smorgasbord Christians. They are types who are "a little of this and some of that, but none of those, thank you, and make certain I am treated right too!" and they have very little endurance or willingness to receive direction or correction. Check it out. The Bible tells you to accept authority. If you are under authority, you then have authority. An ambassador is given imputed authority. He does not carry it except through accreditation. He must be under authority.

Ambassadors derive their accreditation from letters of credence, issued by the head of their state. These internationally recognized documents must be presented to and accepted by foreign heads of state. Without the letter of accreditation, an ambassador has no recognition from the country they serve in. So it is also, with the kingdom of heaven.

> *"But also some of the Jewish exorcists, who went from place to place, attempted to name over those who had the evil spirits the name of the Lord Jesus, saying, "I adjure you by Jesus whom Paul preaches." Seven sons of one Sceva, a Jewish chief priest, were doing this. And the evil spirit answered and said to them, "I recognize Jesus, and I know about Paul, but who are you?" And the man, in whom was the evil spirit, leaped on them and subdued all of them and overpowered them, so that they fled out of that house naked and wounded."*
> Acts 19:13-16

The seven sons came without accreditation. They needed to be under authority in order to have authority. Without it, they were powerless against the governing presence.

Here are some comparisons to the parameters of a natural ambassador and to the one who is sent from the kingdom of God to this kingdom.

First - Ambassadors are appointed and sent to their positions. You are indeed appointed and sent.

"You did not choose Me but I chose you, and appointed you that you would go and bear fruit, and that your fruit would remain, so that whatever you ask of the Father in My name He may give to you."
John 15:16-17

"So Jesus said to them again, "Peace be with you; as the Father has sent Me, I also send you." And when He had said this, He breathed on them and said to them, "Receive the Holy Spirit. "If you forgive the sins of any, their sins have been forgiven them; if you retain the sins of any, they have been retained."
John 20:21-23

"And He said to them, 'Go into all the world and preach the gospel to all creation'."
Mark 16:14-16

It is interesting to note that the "Go" in this statement does not require a physical trip but a spiritual one. There is a "leaving" required. You must leave life as you always lived it and enter a new relationship to the world of which you used to be part.

Second - Ambassadors are plenipotentiary—the word comes from the Latin combination of "plenus"- full, and "potens"-power – becoming "full of power".
You are indeed fully empowered.

"But you will receive power when the Holy Spirit has come upon you; and you shall be My witnesses both in Jerusalem, and in all Judea and Samaria, and even to the remotest part of the earth."
Acts 1:8

Chapter 7

Third—   Ambassadors must be accredited.
You are indeed accredited.

"Truly, truly, I say to you, he who believes in Me, the works that I do, he will do also; and greater works than these he will do; because I go to the Father. "Whatever you ask in My name, that will I do, so that the Father may be glorified in the Son. "If you ask Me anything in My name, I will do it."
John 14:12-14

"For we are His workmanship, created in Christ Jesus for good works, which God prepared beforehand so that we would walk in them."
Ephesians 2:10

Fourth—   Ambassadors enjoy complete diplomatic immunity.
You are indeed afforded diplomatic immunity.

"For the law of the Spirit of life in Christ Jesus has set you free from the law of sin and of death. For what the Law could not do, weak as it was through the flesh, God did: sending His own Son in the likeness of sinful flesh and as an offering for sin, He condemned sin in the flesh, so that the requirement of the Law might be fulfilled in us, who do not walk according to the flesh but according to the Spirit."
Romans 8:2-5

When you walk in the spirit, you are no longer under the law of sin and death. Your role and position in the kingdom has set you free from the laws that govern this kingdom of darkness.

> *"If you have died with Christ to the elementary principles of the world, why, as if you were living in the world, do you submit yourself to decrees, such as, "Do not handle, do not taste, do not touch!" (Which all refer to things destined to perish with use)—in accordance with the commandments and teachings of men."*
> Colossians 2:20-23

However, I must clarify here. If you believe you are still under those laws and respond to life as if you are, then you don't enjoy the benefit of your role and position. If you don't recognize your separation from this world, and instead conform to the lifestyle of those whose culture you are meant to be in but not of, then you will fall under their laws. The entire second chapter of Colossians has much to do with your favored status as a kingdom citizen, so if you still have questions about this, get a Bible out and read the whole chapter.

Fifth— Ambassadors must be sent by the head-of-state.

The one who has sent you indeed has been given the head-of-state status.

> *"And Jesus came up and spoke to them, saying, "All authority has been given to Me in heaven and on earth. " Go therefore and make disciples of all the nations, baptizing them in the name of the Father and the Son and the Holy Spirit, teaching them to observe all that I commanded you; and lo, I am with you always, even to the end of the age."*
> Matthew 28:18-20

Because Jesus had been given all authority, He had the authority to send you, and send you He did. The question is not "Have you been sent?" The question is "Have you gone?"

At this point I am sure you are seeing the significance of the calling of God to those of His kingdom. The similarities between an ambassador of a worldly kingdom and our ambassadorship for the kingdom of God here on this earth are quite clear. For myself, it was a clarification that has helped me respond to Jesus' request to "go into all the world," recognizing that I am appointed to represent my kingdom and live as an alien in the land I am sent to represent God's kingdom to.

Now let's imagine a scenario similar to the one with which we started this chapter.

You are sitting in your home and the phone rings. Someone in your home answers it and then hands the phone to you. With an incredulous look on their face, they say, "It's for you and it's the Lord." I would imagine a number of questioning thoughts would go through your mind as you reached for the phone. (Besides wondering why the Lord would use a phone, that is.)

In this scenario, there are quite a few who are willing to put this caller on hold. However, let's suppose you got over your shock He would use such a way to contact you, and you listened intently as He said "I would like to have you represent the kingdom of God to another kingdom and I am appointing you as my ambassador."

Your immediate thought might be, "I'm not qualified!" Or "I can't!" From that point, this should at least follow the same path of how one would respond to the President. Instead, I personally know many who have responded, "I have more important things to do. Maybe some other time. I have a camping trip planned, not to mention my golf tournament on Sunday."

Still, the Lord continues. "I know who you are and have determined you have the qualities I need. I will give you time to equip yourself and I will provide you with the information you need so you can study to show yourself approved. After sufficient time to prepare you are to "go" and represent me. You will be afforded all the honor and power that goes with your position. In addition to giving you the position, I have adopted you as my child so you will go bearing my name and lineage. You may freely make use of my name to accomplish the purposes for which I am sending you. Since I am placing my name upon you, you will be fully accredited. I will provide all the support you need and will give you my special envoy, the Holy Spirit, as your helper and to be with you wherever you go. Anything for which you ask in my name I will give it. I personally will handle all of your requests and I have already made certain you have what material you need to prepare. I have given you my bible and in it you will find everything you need to make your way prosperous and have good success. I have also given you, as gifts, my servants—apostles, prophets, evangelists, pastors and teachers, whose role it is to prepare my children for the work of the ministry to which I called them. They will help you as well. You will represent Me and my Kingdom to the kingdom of darkness and declare My praises so that the citizens of that kingdom might come to know My nature.

Would you tell the Lord "No"? The answer to that one is not so clear. Sadly, many say "No way!" I think that most who say "No" do so out of ignorance about the high calling of Christ. They have little understanding of the power which the kingdom has available to them or even how to tap into it. Also, they wonder—if the kingdom where they are to be sent has rejected the head-of-state of the kingdom of heaven—Jesus—how much more will His ambassadors be rejected? They desire the approval of man more than the approval of God, and so they decline. Upon declining, they satisfy themselves by attending meetings and having share-a-dishes and going to concerts and seminars and a lot of the same activities a kingdom Christian would do. And yet, they do little with the position and privilege that the Lord calls them to.

I would ask you to consider the honor the Lord bestows on His children as kingdom representatives and answer "Yes". What "yes" actually means to you is that you will begin to live your life from the perspective of one who is called according to His purposes and you will begin to see your role in life though your appointed calling. If you answer "Yes", you will live alongside of the citizens of the kingdom of darkness, but will understand you are doing so in order to represent your head-of-state to them. You will look for opportunities to do this, though you won't make a nuisance of yourself in so doing. You will live in their neighborhoods, but not live the way they live. Mainly, you will maintain a life of great testimony so that when you do have the opportunity to present your kingdom and represent the King, it won't be discredited by how you have been living your life. If you will represent the one who has called you and be diligent in your role as ambassador for the kingdom, when you stand before Him you will receive the words: "Well done, good and faithful servant. You have been faithful in little, I will make you ruler over much."

> "But you are a chosen race, a royal priesthood, a holy nation, a people for God's own possession, so that you may proclaim the excellencies of Him who has called you out of darkness into His marvelous light; for you once were not a people, but now you are the people of God; you had not received mercy, but now you have received mercy."
> 1 Peter 2:9-11

Intermission

I would like to take a moment in this book to allow you to pause and reflect on what has gone before and what lies ahead. The kingdom of God is the course and direction that is laid before every born again believer. It is what was purchased for you. It is a kingdom filled with God's promises. A kingdom filled with power. It exists here and now and will be coming in greater visibility and glory on this earth at the end of this age. It is built upon the supernatural power of God. Your citizenship in it is assured through spiritual birth. It is where the promise land lies. Everything after you get saved and before you enter the kingdom is simply wilderness.

Egypt:

Egypt represents this world—the kingdom our enemy, Satan, rules. It is a kingdom of captivity and slavery—addiction and bad habits—pain and suffering mixed with indulgence and pleasure. It is a kingdom of darkness. Its citizens are born blind at natural birth and their path is the path of death. Death permeates everything in it. Even the pleasant things of that kingdom carry with them the sentence of death. It is a land of broken promises and wounded hearts. Every man woman and child is born into this dreadful kingdom but many escape. It is a good place to escape from; it's a good place from which to become expatriated. The only way to do that is to obtain a new citizenship through birth—the birth of your spirit.

The Wilderness:

The wilderness is a place where God provides for you but is not meant to be a place of residence. It is that no-mans-land which lies between the Egypt of this world's kingdom and the promise of God's kingdom. Manna is in the wilderness. Water is in the wilderness. Even experiences with God are in the wilderness but power is not found in the wilderness. The wilderness is a place to learn about your new citizenship and the kingdom you are traveling to. It is a place to pass through—not a place to live. Every new citizen must pass through it, but sadly many simply set up residence there, refusing to cross the Jordan until they die. You are meant to cross the wilderness, by faith step into the Jordan River at flood stage believing God to make a way for you, and enter the promised land in this life. If you are a wilderness dweller, this book is meant to encourage you to fold up your dwelling and lead you to where you are supposed to be going. If you are a saint already on your journey or simply beginning your travels to the kingdom, it is meant to give you signposts for that narrow path that leads there. Unless you are already a kingdom resident and were already aware of those things of which I've written, then you are either traveling through or need to travel through the wilderness to your new place of residence. Knowing about the kingdom won't bring you there. Entering it is not automatic in this life. You must make the effort needed to pass through the wilderness in order to get there.

The wilderness is the place of the "natural" meeting the "spiritual". It is not a spiritual place though spiritual things might take place there. You have what you see in the wilderness, though you are trying to learn to see with your spiritual eyes. You survive partly on what God provides and partly on what you do—mainly because you haven't learned how to walk in God's total provision yet. God is a column of smoke by day and fire by night and you rely on your senses to follow Him as you go forward. But soon—so very soon if you don't give up, you can cross your Jordan River into the promised land of the kingdom.

Intermission

The Promised Land:

This kingdom you are going to is different than Egypt in many ways. It has different principles and different ways of functioning. Much of the tactics you have adapted in order to cope with the Egypt you came from will need to be thrown away so you can adapt to your new surroundings. You will not need a visa to enter, because you carry a kingdom passport, since you have become one of its citizens.

It has a few restrictions. You cannot live there as you have always lived. You cannot bring your old culture with you. It is NOT multicultural in this sense. You will need to learn its language and its laws. Its laws are different than the laws of this world and your surroundings are defined in different terms. It is not a land where you can use your natural senses, for it is spiritually experienced. It will not let you walk with your eyes, or sense with your feelings. Those are the tools through which the prince of this world's kingdom confuses and misleads his captives. You will need to learn to walk in your faith and see with your spirit. You will feel but disregard any feelings that exult themselves against the knowledge of Christ. You will be clothed with the power of the Spirit. You will only do those things the Father tells you to do.

The kingdom is a land where the fruit is so huge it is carried between two men on poles and it is flowing with milk and honey. It is a land where giants topple and armies flee before you. Where cities fall at a shout and you walk through the waters and He is with you and through the rivers and they do not overflow you. In this new land you walk through the fire and don't get burned, neither does the flame kindle upon you. God goes out before you and drives out your enemies and fear fades away behind the glory of the One you walk with. It is a place of power and love—a place of peace and joy. A place where your burdens are light and your yoke is easy. It is a place for entering God's rest and basking in the royalty of God's appointment and the joy of Jesus' presence. It is a land of promise and purpose. It is the land to which you gained citizenship when you accepted Jesus. It is a land which leads to your inheritance.

Does this sound like the land you intended to find? Do you want what this "kingdom of God" has to offer? Then take a deep breath and press forward. Grab a sandwich, a cold glass of something non-alcoholic, a comfortable chair, and read on. You will learn that if you persevere in your Christian walk, if you endure through trials in your life, the Spirit will lead you to this Promised Land—this Kingdom of God.

"Do not be afraid, little flock, for your Father has chosen gladly to give you the kingdom."
Luke 12:32

Chapter 8
Walking in all your Citizenship Provides

"And Jesus came up and spoke to them, saying, 'All authority has been given to Me in heaven and on earth.'"
Matthew 28:18

What if you were given the right to command all the powers of the universe? What if you could tell the kingdom of darkness where to go? What if you could have anything for which you asked? What if you could say to a mountain "Be taken up and cast into the sea," and it would do it? What if the demons themselves would have to obey you?

Sounds pretty unbelievable doesn't it? Well, the Bible says you can have just that! If you are a carnal thinker, the scriptures I will place before you in this chapter will challenge your ability to believe. Many have read these and concluded they were not meant for them, though nothing in the content limits their use to a select few. To those with faith, these scriptures have relevance. Each scripture has limitations though. Those limitations mostly relate to the spiritual mind set of the believer.

The world often hands you a title and a job, but doesn't give you the power to enforce. In the kingdom of God you are not given responsibility without authority. Whom God sends, He equips. Keep this quotation in mind, "God doesn't call people who are qualified. He calls people who are willing and then He qualifies them." (Richard Parker) He is able to abundantly supply you with power for the task to which He calls you.

"Now to Him who is able to do far more abundantly beyond all that we ask or think, according to the power that works within us,"
Ephesians 3:20

Chapter 8

"In that day you will not question Me about anything. Truly, truly, I say to you, if you ask the Father for anything in My name, He will give it to you. Until now you have asked for nothing in My name; ask and you will receive, so that your joy may be made full."
John 16:23-24

"Truly, truly, I say to you, he who believes in Me, the works that I do, he will do also; and greater works than these he will do; because I go to the Father. Whatever you ask in My name, that will I do, so that the Father may be glorified in the Son. If you ask Me anything in My name, I will do it."
John 14:12-14

And Jesus answered and said to them, "Truly I say to you, if you have faith and do not doubt, you will not only do what was done to the fig tree, but even if you say to this mountain, 'Be taken up and cast into the sea,' it will happen. And all things you ask in prayer, believing, you will receive."
Matthew 21:21-22

And He said to them, "Go into all the world and preach the gospel to all creation. He who has believed and has been baptized shall be saved; but he who has disbelieved shall be condemned. These signs will accompany those who believe: in My name they will cast out demons, they will speak with new tongues; they will pick up serpents, and if they drink any deadly poison, it will not hurt them; they will lay hands on the sick, and they will recover."
Mark 16:14-18

The seventy returned with joy, saying, "Lord, even the demons are subject to us in Your name." And He said to them, "I was watching Satan fall from heaven like lightning. Behold, I have given you authority to tread on serpents and scorpions, and over all the

power of the enemy, and nothing will injure you. Nevertheless do not rejoice in this, that the spirits are subject to you, but rejoice that your names are recorded in heaven."
Luke 10:17-20

Do you believe these scriptures? Do you believe they apply to you? If you believe they don't apply to you, you have entered a slippery slope with no way down. You are left with the difficult task of determining which, if any, of the Bible's scriptures apply to you. Do the scriptures which relate to God providing for your daily needs apply to you? Maybe you can't count on God to provide a way for you to have your daily needs met. Many don't believe you can. How about those scriptures granting forgiveness for sins? Maybe your sins aren't forgiven? Maybe, if these scriptures I listed can't be applied to you, then maybe those other scriptures you've been hanging onto can't be relied on either. You are then left with an empty religion with simple acts which must be preformed without power. You recite, you attend, you follow, you chant, you pray, you sing songs, but you live your life just like everyone else and you hope you go to heaven when you die. You hope the resurrection applies to you. You hope you spend eternity with Christ. But you never really know and when you die, you die scared.

If that is the path you choose, then pick your religion based upon the rituals you enjoy and go to the grave with no real hope. I have known many people who have done just that. My request to you is, choose to believe the Bible in all its glory. The Bible says it is all inspired by God and all profitable for teaching, for reproof, for correction, for training in righteousness; so the man of God may be adequate, equipped for every good work. (2 Timothy 3:16-17) You should choose to believe the Timothy scripture. You need to believe if your experiences don't match the Bible, then there is a problem in you, and you need to discover what it is so you can move into what God has purchased for you. God says "You will find me when you seek me with all your heart." Jesus says "Seek first the kingdom of

Chapter 8

God." Though sometimes the kingdom seems elusive in its power, if you will set aside the things which distract, and pursue God with all that is in you, you can have the experiences the Bible describes as part of a disciples life. You must simply choose to obey rather than delay.

Mark 16:17 says, "These signs will accompany those who believe." It is the believing the signs will "accompany" which opens the door for the power. The signs accompany those who believe they will accompany them. Jesus went to His home town and could do no great miracles because of their unbelief. That was Jesus. Even His power was made impotent by the unbelief of those to whom He came. It is the same with you and me. If we don't believe we have power, then we don't have power. If we believe we can have the power, we may still not have the power, but we are able to move into it if we rid ourselves of those things which drain us of the power that could be ours. The one is a situation without repair unless a change of mind occurs, but the other is totally redeemable.

If, as you are reading this, you begin to feel defeated, take heart. No situation in Christianity is without redemption. You can "choose" to believe and thus begin to move into that belief. "You of little faith" is how Jesus often referred to His disciples, yet they were able to begin the church, the force that changed the world. History is impacted by her (the church), the calendar established because of her, and the whole world is brought to an uproar by her. All of this because 120 stout hearted believers chose to go to Jerusalem and wait to be clothed with power. They expected it. They longed for it. They believed in it. So should you.

If you believe God for your salvation, shouldn't you also believe God for the power to accomplish mighty exploits? Shouldn't you believe you can indeed do all things through Christ who strengthens you? That God has called you and who He calls He also equips? That if you lay hands on the sick they will recover? That if you were in need of having a mountain removed you could get the job done by speaking at it? That you should be able to do greater works then Jesus did? That if you ask anything of the Father in Jesus' name it will be done for you? That He is able to do far more abundantly beyond all we ask or think, according to the power which works within us?

I want you to recall two incidents in which Jesus rebuked His disciples:

Matthew 8:23-27

Christ had been ministering with his disciples in a community called Capernaum on the northwest end of the Sea of Galilee. He decided to go to the southeast side and got into a boat with His disciples. Since the testimony Jesus gives is that He only did what the Father told Him to do, we know He was going across to do the Father's bidding. As they sailed south and east to cross the inland sea, a rather intense storm arose. Keep in mind, of the twelve, over a fourth of them were from a fishing background. They knew this sea and knew storms and knew when you were in trouble and when you were not. Us land lubbers might think we were in trouble if the boat rocked a little, but these guys were seasoned fishermen. If they thought they were close to perishing, it has credibility. Finally, they could stand it no longer. They went to the Father's son and woke Him. Now at this point, my thinking is that my response would be, "Why didn't you wake me sooner? Let's get some buckets and start bailing." At the very least, I would have thought He would have something positive to say like, "Well, you certainly waited a good long time to panic. Way to go boys!" Instead, His response was, "Why are you so afraid?" I can hear some of us today saying, "Cause, like, the boat is sinking!"

Chapter 8

Matthew 14:28-33

In this account, the disciples were in a boat by themselves. Jesus had just fed the five thousand, sent His disciples across to Capernaum ahead of Him and then had gone off to pray. He, just that day, received the news that His cousin, John, had been beheaded. It was night and again a storm arose. Not as bad as the previous storm, but the disciples had only been able to row the boat a few miles when they saw Jesus walking on the water out to them. Once they got over their initial shock, Peter asked Jesus to call for him to come out to Him on the water. Jesus does just that, and Peter gets out of the boat and begins to walk across the water. When I first read this I thought, "Wow! What awesome faith Peter showed! Getting out of a boat in the middle of the sea in the middle of the night in the middle of the storm! That takes more than just a middle-of-the-road faith!" Along the way, the storm again reclaims Peter's attention and he begins to sink. Now keep in mind, sinking in water is pretty normal. If you were to step out of a boat I think you will be lucky to take two steps before you're treading water. Yet this display was not impressive to Jesus. His response was, "You of little faith, why did you doubt?"

These accounts tell me something about God's attitude toward believing. He expects us to. He is not very impressed when we don't. In each of these incidents, there is very good natural reason to be afraid. As a matter of fact, fear would seem to be the proper natural response as it prepares one for action, and it would seem action was needed in both instances. Jesus' reaction was, they should have remained at rest. These stories are more than just accounts. They are related for our benefit that we might learn and so that the man of God may be adequate, equipped for every good work. They show us the mind of Christ and His attitude toward this world around us. They teach us what our real and reactive response is supposed to be. If this isn't our response, then we have some work to do. But then that's what this book is all about, isn't it? I don't believe we have begun to walk in the faith that a kingdom walk is supposed to be built on. In the next chapter I will focus entirely on the faith the kingdom is built on and resting in that faith.

I would like to establish a truth for you, to help you believe in the power which can be yours. Jesus has all the authority. He has removed Satan's authority. He has authority over life and death. The bible says, "All authority in heaven and earth has been given to Jesus." Jesus wasn't the only one who declared this. It is spoken about by many writers in the bible:

John the Baptist:
"The Father loves the Son and has given all things into His hand."
John 3:35

David the psalmist:
"You make him to rule over the works of Your hands; You have put all things under his feet,"
Psalms 8:6

Paul:
"These are in accordance with the working of the strength of His might which He brought about in Christ, when He raised Him from the dead and seated Him at His right hand in the heavenly places, far above all rule and authority and power and dominion, and every name that is named, not only in this age but also in the one to come. And He put all things in subjection under His feet, and gave Him as head over all things to the church, which is His body, the fullness of Him who fills all in all."
Ephesians 1:19-23

Chapter 8

The writer of the book to the Hebrews quotes David in reference to Jesus:

"'...You have put all things in subjection under His feet.' For in subjecting all things to him, He left nothing that is not subject to him. But now we do not yet see all things subjected to him."
Hebrews 2:8

Peter:
"Corresponding to that, baptism now saves you—not the removal of dirt from the flesh, but an appeal to God for a good conscience—through the resurrection of Jesus Christ, who is at the right hand of God, having gone into heaven, after angels and authorities and powers had been subjected to Him."
1 Peter 3:21-22

God is infinite in His knowledge and infinite in His Power. He knows the end from the beginning and nothing is hidden from Him. Since he has all knowledge and all power, wouldn't it seem to make sense to put your trust in such a being? Shouldn't you choose life over death? Shouldn't you choose power over impotence? Shouldn't you choose to believe rather than disbelieve?

I have seen many people who want to believe these truths, begin to act on them and then nothing happens in their experiences that they can look at, point to, and say "look at what I did!" It is the "I did" concept which kills their power. Ownership is not allowed. In the kingdom of God, everything belongs to God. The power, the glory, the earth and all that is in it. As long as God retains the ownership, the power to do His will remains. As soon as you make it yours, the power disappears. What you do, you must do for and through God and the glory must belong to Him. I realize I need to clarify this so let me give you a scenario which happens very often in a kingdom-minded Christian's life.

Let's suppose God gives you a project to do in the kingdom. Maybe He gives you a vision for a business He wants established to advance the kingdom, maybe a ministry to your community, maybe even just a ministry in the church. You've become a kingdom Christian, so you know that your time and efforts belong to the kingdom. As you seek God for your part in the kingdom, He shows you what He has in mind and you begin to be obedient to the vision. You pour yourself into it, endeavoring to do a good job. No problem so far. You struggle along, praying often, and seeking God for direction. You ask for those things which are essential to accomplish the task, and often they naturally seem to appear. Many times, however, you are intimately involved in making them appear. Maybe you talk with a financial source that suddenly sees the value in your vision. Maybe you find a way to raise capital through the sale of some asset or another. You believe God is leading you and you pour these things and your energy into the vision God has given you. Much of your blood, sweat, and tears go into causing this 'thing' to come to pass. You become invested in it. Up to this point you have not yet sinned, but the pieces are in place which could cause you to sin and the enemy is well aware of the power which could be yours if you don't. Therefore, he intervenes. He tempts you to revert to carnal thinking. A problem presents itself as an obstacle to the vision God has given you. You remember the effort which was called for in order to overcome the last obstacle, and though you realize there were some supernatural powers working on your behalf back then, you decide to own the effort you put into that problem. Since so much of you was involved in the solution, you now become the reason the solution came about. You take ownership. Since you now begin to think you were the reason that solution was accomplished, you now become the power to solve the new problem. However, power is not something you own. Apart from Christ you can do nothing. Real fear and trepidation comes up here, and it should. What if you can't pull it off? What if all your efforts don't accomplish the goal? Unfortunately you are so invested in the vision at this time, there is no way you can give it up, and so you begin to 'own' it. You must maintain it at all costs. It becomes a reflection of you. "If it fails, you've failed" is your thinking. Now you have sinned. You begin to thrash around in your life, trying hard to keep this 'thing' going. Your belief system has shifted from, "I will trust God" to "it depends on me." You move from a place of rest to a place of fear. Many reasons for fear assail you and you give in to them.

You have come to a crossroad. If you continue down the road you are on, disappointment, disillusionment, disheartening, and many other 'dis' things await you. You become very vulnerable here. You will begin to hear the enemy say, "I thought God told you He would be with you?" "Did God say. . . ?" frames itself often in your thinking. If you give in to these suggestions, you will begin to give up and believe the lie that will come next. "See? You can't have faith that God will deliver you." This is the trap the enemy lays for those who would do the will of the Father. It is one of unbelief. It is not faith.

When you find yourself in this place, I want you to remember the story about Abraham. (Genesis 15-23) He needed an heir and asked God for one. God promised him an heir and Abraham waited for the promise. He gave up waiting and decided to solve the problem himself. Instead of solving the problem, he created one. God fulfilled the promise and he now had the promised son and the problem son he created. Wouldn't it have been nice if he only had the promised son?

However, Abraham was able to learn from the problem he created and he decided he would, in the future, own nothing but obedience in faith. When God said to Abraham, "I want you to sacrifice your son, your only begotten son," he did not thrash around trying to keep it going through creative problem solving. He obediently went up the mountain and prepared to sacrifice his vision. So must you. It is imperative that you do not own the work you do. It is for God and it belongs to Him, not you.

When you are faced with a seemingly insurmountable problem between you and accomplishing the vision God has put before you, you must surrender to the will of God and when you have done all, simply stand and wait for the Father. You must be willing to say, "none the less, not my will but Your will be done." That is where there is power. It is the power of the resurrection.

> *"But whatever things were gain to me, those things I have counted as loss for the sake of Christ. More than that, I count all things to be loss in view of the surpassing value of knowing Christ Jesus my Lord, for whom I have suffered the loss of all things, and count them but rubbish so that I may gain Christ, and may be found in Him, not having a righteousness of my own derived from the Law, but that which is through faith in Christ, the righteousness which comes from God on the basis of faith, that I may know Him and the power of His resurrection and the fellowship of His sufferings, being conformed to His death; in order that I may attain to the resurrection from the dead."*
> *Philippians 3:7-11*

When you come to your Gethsemane experience in your kingdom walk, it will feel much like death. That's because it is. You will at this point begin to understand the passage which says:

> *"For whoever wishes to save his life will lose it; but whoever loses his life for My sake will find it."*
> *Matthew 16:25*

This passage has little relevance apart from kingdom-mindedness. If everything you are doing in life is all about you and your retirement, your new home, your new car and what you will eat and what you will drink and what you will put on, then there really is nothing to 'gain'. You are pursuing your goals and you have them. The problem is there is no "power" in those goals. You are at the mercy of your economic conditions, and they can go up in smoke in an instant. The sad part is that your loss won't even have gain attached. It will simply be loss.

> "Peter began to say to Him, 'Behold, we have left everything and followed You.' Jesus said, 'Truly I say to you, there is no one who has left house or brothers or sisters or mother or father or children or farms, for My sake and for the gospel's sake, but that he will receive a hundred times as much now in the present age, houses and brothers and sisters and mothers and children and farms, along with persecutions; and in the age to come, eternal life.'"
> Mark 10:28-31

In this passage Jesus talks about loss in reference to the gospel of the kingdom. (The disciples were taught to preach the gospel of the kingdom. We also are told to preach the gospel of the kingdom.) "This gospel of the kingdom shall be preached in the whole world as a testimony to all the nations, and then the end will come." (Matthew 24:14) If the loss is for the kingdom, there is no loss. If the loss is you losing as you pursue your own purposes in life, it's just loss. The promise to make all things work out (Romans 8:28) does not include ownership of your universe. You must give it up in order to obtain these promises. The point however, is that in giving it up, you obtain enormous power to use as God wishes it to be used, and you can be very effective against our adversary, the devil.

When you walk in that type of kingdom surrender, you will lay hands on the sick and they will recover. The lame will walk. The dead will be raised. Mountains will be moved. You will see the power of God work on your behalf first hand. Many will come to know Him and your message will be delivered with signs and wonders following. None of it will be for show. None of it will bring glory to you. You will have no ownership in it and your testimony will be that of Jesus, who said, "I only do those things the father has asked me to do."

> *"I can do nothing on My own initiative. As I hear, I judge; and My judgment is just, because I do not seek My own will, but the will of Him who sent Me."*
> *John 5:30*

Chapter 9
Finding "Rest" in the Kingdom

"You foolish Galatians, who has bewitched you, before whose eyes Jesus Christ was publicly portrayed as crucified? This is the only thing I want to find out from you: did you receive the Spirit by the works of the Law, or by hearing with faith? Are you so foolish? Having begun by the Spirit, are you now being perfected by the flesh? Did you suffer so many things in vain—if indeed it was in vain? So then, does He who provides you with the Spirit and works miracles among you, do it by the works of the Law, or by hearing with faith?"
Galatians 3:1-5

How appalling it was for Paul to find that the people of Galatia had moved from a vibrant faith walk of power and action into a dry religious experience which had become 'works' based. For many Christians, knowing God is less about faith and more about duty. Their attendance at church defines their Christian experience and their awareness of their faith often ends at the sanctuary door. They carefully—or not so carefully—abide by a set of rules and regulations and think that somehow they have made God happy with their lifeless sacrifices. They pay their tithes because it's proper, they attend the services because it's expected, they serve in Sunday school or greet at the door or serve in some fashion because that's what's expected of Christians. They smile, the say all the right things, they don't swear, they quit as many bad habits as they are able, and somehow that becomes "Christianity" for them. Their works define their faith rather than their faith energizing their works. True, it feels pretty hollow, but then isn't that what everyone is doing?

Chapter 9

While they receive some benefit from their "Churchianity," the real benefits of true "life," which are there for the kingdom citizens, are not experienced by them. Our Christian church culture rewards such "Churchianity". It does not create problems and it allows the local church organization to go forward with little difficulty. Since the fortressed church is made full by such activity, these types of Christians are regarded as pretty good saints. Since this level of faith is non-threatening, more and more friends join this "church" and these works-based saints are considered very productive. They will be given honor and recognition for their efforts, which will appeal to their flesh, and they will endeavor harder and harder to receive more and more such pleasant experiences. They will again become pursuers of comfort and security within the confines of the church, albeit a false security and an external comfort. These types of people will often be referred to as spiritual, though little spirituality is involved. They will wave the flags the hardest, they will dance the most, they will use Christian euphemisms more often, and they will give more testimonies, teach many classes, and, to a new believer, seem quite impressive. The new believer begins to emulate those who are called spiritual and convinces himself that this truly defines spirituality and this anomaly of Christianity propagates itself again and again until it becomes the norm.

On the other hand, real Christianity is nothing like a carnal experience. Rewards are eternal, not temporal, and often times the immediate experience one has is of rejection and dismissal. If you are looking for good feelings alone, then the true faith walk is not for you. You can't even take pride in being led by the Spirit, because then you commit the sin of pride and immediately become led by the flesh again. A true faith walk requires practice, because it is truly a narrow road which will require all of your balance to remain on it. However, if you are looking for the supernatural manifestation of God, then your walk must become one of pure faith and your Christianity must become real kingdom Christianity. Your satisfaction in life must be in pleasing the Father and not men—in obedience and not self-promotion.

Many people who say they trust God don't really trust God at all. Their idea about faith is to have faith He will do what they want. Unfortunately, this leads to disillusionment and distrust in God, because God won't do what you want. You call on Him to deliver you in some way or another, and when He doesn't do what you've asked, you choose to become offended and give in to the temptation that says, "God can't be trusted."

I like the account in Daniel 3 about Shadrach, Meshach and Abednego. When faced with the fiery furnace, they told the king, "If we are thrown into the blazing furnace, the God whom we serve is able to save us. He will rescue us from your power [one way or another], Your Majesty. But even if he doesn't [deliver us from the furnace], Your Majesty can be sure that we will never serve your gods or worship the gold statue you have set up." They weren't committed to a particular deliverance. They knew that they would not be in the power of the king no matter which way it went, and they did not confine God to one way of delivering them. Whether they died in the flames and went to Abraham's bosom, or whether God miraculously preserved them, or delivered them some other way, they knew their God could be trusted.

Charles S. Price wrote a good book about faith called <u>The Real Faith</u>. In it he compared the difference between presumption and faith. It is presumptuous to suppose we can dictate to God those things which we desire to have come to pass and simply by believing strongly enough, force Him to do our will. To many, God has become that great sugar-daddy in the sky and they get offended when He doesn't deliver to them according to their plan.

Chapter 9

God is the designer of our destiny. Many factors go into how He designs each and every destiny, but the design is His and only His. Faith is discovering what His destiny is for you and working in cooperation with God to bring it to pass. In the midst of dismal circumstances that seem to crush your dreams, faith is trusting that God has designed a good outcome to the bad circumstances. It doesn't restrict the outcome to a specific set of circumstances, but trusts that all things work together for good since you are called to His purposes and to love the Lord.

I have a saying I use constantly: "If you can see how it will work out, then it's not faith." Only when the circumstances are so convincingly hopeless and it is evident there is no conceivable way for things to work out, only then can you truly begin to walk in faith. What a joy it is then, when trouble comes. It allows your faith to grow, along with perseverance, faithfulness, integrity and all of those qualities that mark a true kingdom Christian. You can truly praise God for bringing those times that leave you no temptation to trust in what you see, since there is nothing good to see. You can thank God He has brought you into a time that will allow you to please Him.

> "But without faith it is impossible to please Him, for he who comes to God must believe that He is, and that He is a rewarder of those who diligently seek Him."
> Hebrews 11:6

You begin to see what Christianity is meant to be when you discover faith. It is obedience based on hope, which is given substance by faith. He says "the righteous ones will live by their faith."

> "Behold, as for the proud one, his soul is not right within him; But the righteous will live by his faith."
> Habakkuk 2:4

That scripture says it all. When you live by your own power, you are living in pride and your soul suffers. Only when you humble yourself and rely on God can He lift you up. Only then can you experience rest. Until that time, you will struggle with fear and discontent. You will clamor and become uneasy. You will get out of balance, putting more of you into something than is required and using your time unwisely. Your days will be tense and your relationships will suffer. If you have a spouse or children, they will feel the brunt of your neglect. Jesus says His yoke is easy. His burden is light. That only happens in the kingdom of God. When you live by kingdom principles, 'rest' will be your Christian experience. Here is the rest I am talking about:

"Therefore, let us fear if, while a promise remains of entering His rest, any one of you may seem to have come short of it. For indeed we have had good news preached to us, just as they also; but the word they heard did not profit them, because it was not united by faith in those who heard. For we who have believed enter that rest, just as He has said,"
Hebrews 4:1-3

"So there remains a Sabbath rest for the people of God. For the one who has entered His rest has himself also rested from his works, as God did from His. Therefore let us be diligent to enter that rest, so that no one will fall, through following the same example of disobedience. For the word of God is living and active and sharper than any two-edged sword, and piercing as far as the division of soul and spirit, of both joints and marrow, and able to judge the thoughts and intentions of the heart."
Hebrews 4:9-13

These verses from Hebrews speak about entering a 'rest'. In chapter three, the writer of the letter to the Hebrews compared this to Israel's crossing of the wilderness out of Egypt and going to the Promised Land. In that account, twelve men went to look at the land God had promised them. All twelve went to the same place, saw the same things, and experienced the same experiences. Ten men saw only the problems and measured their own ability to solve them. Two men saw the blessings and measured God's ability to give the land to them. The two who saw the blessings and dismissed the problems because of God's ability to solve them eventually went in. The ten who only saw the problems and measured their ability to solve them, never entered that Promised Land.

> *"Then Caleb quieted the people before Moses and said, 'We should by all means go up and take possession of it, for we will surely overcome it.' But the men who had gone up with him said, 'We are not able to go up against the people, for they are too strong for us.' So they gave out to the sons of Israel a bad report of the land which they had spied out, saying, 'The land through which we have gone, in spying it out, is a land that devours its inhabitants; and all the people whom we saw in it are men of great size. There also we saw the Nephilim (the sons of Anak are part of the Nephilim); and we became like grasshoppers in our own sight, and so we were in their sight.'"*
> Numbers 13:30-33

Negative viewpoints are attributed to unbelief in this passage. "So we see that they were not able to enter because of unbelief" (Hebrews 3:19). If you believe God is with you and has called you to accomplish a purpose for Him in the kingdom of God, then problems only become opportunities to see God move in your behalf. This is what kingdom Christianity is all about. If you are a citizen of the kingdom, you're called according to HIS purposes, not your own. Therefore, if God is for you, who in the world can be against you (Read Romans 8)? What do you have to fear? Of course, all of this rests on the premise you have given up your control and put God in control. Such "giving up control" is a "belief" that God is for you. God is who He says He is and He can indeed be trusted! Hebrews 11:6 states that in order to please God you must believe that He is who He says and that He will reward those who diligently seek Him.

Jesus told two kingdom parables about this fact.

"The kingdom of heaven is like a treasure hidden in the field, which a man found and hid again; and from joy over it he goes and sells all that he has and buys that field."

"Again, the kingdom of heaven is like a merchant seeking fine pearls, and upon finding one pearl of great value, he went and sold all that he had and bought it."
Matthew 13:44-46

I wish I could tell you there was an easy way to enter the kingdom of God, but then it wouldn't be valuable, would it? Jesus spent much time comparing the kingdom of God to principles we could understand. Both of these parables tell the story of cost and value. It is the law of kingdom supply and demand. If you believe in the value God gives to His kingdom, and if you believe what the bible says about the value of a citizenship to that kingdom, then the price is certainly worth it. However, that value will always be brought into question by your enemy. If Satan can convince you God can't be trusted and the trials you face are a result of God's negligence, then you will not find the price palatable enough to pay it.

There is a saying I have heard often; "Salvation is free but discipleship will cost you your life." I am not sure who originated the saying, but it is accurate and based on scripture. Jesus says that unless you were willing to give up your life you could not be His disciple. "So then, none of you can be my disciple who does not give up all his own possessions." (Luke 14:33) You must become a disciple to enter the kingdom of God. A convert doesn't enter until they become a disciple. The cost of entry is "all that you have" according to these two parables. Not everyone will be willing to pay that price, but I am convinced of this. The cost does not exceed the value. It is not overpriced.

Please be assured. I am not speaking of a vow of poverty. I am talking about ownership. Your life is what God gives you as your life. If living as a Christian requires that you hang on to any and all comforts which you currently enjoy, you will never enter the kingdom. If your life must have a certain outcome on a day to day basis, you will not enter the kingdom. If you must enjoy a certain climate in order to be happy, you will not enter the kingdom. If you must have the respect of all around you, you will not enter the kingdom because you cannot serve God and man. The kingdom is all about God and what He wants and not at all about you taking care of you. Let God take care of you and you take care of seeking the kingdom. It seems I remember someone saying something like that once. "Seek first the kingdom of God and all these things will be added to you." Do the first things first and rest in the promise of what follows. Let God be the determiner of "all things" and let Him cause them to "be added to you." Are you beginning to understand what Jesus meant by this statement?

> *"Enter through the narrow gate; for the gate is wide and the way is broad that leads to destruction, and there are many who enter through it." For the gate is small and the way is narrow that leads to life, and there are few who find it."*
> *Matthew 7:13-14*

While I think many have used this scripture to relate to the saved and the unsaved, I think it has a more broad application relating to those who enter the kingdom and those who don't. Death will finally separate you from your body of sin and you will enter the kingdom rather automatically if you're saved. But I believe the "Seek first the kingdom" statement Jesus makes is talking about the kingdom in this life, and the narrow path leads you to the life of the kingdom here in this world. I believe your destiny lies on the very narrow path and your willingness to walk on it. Salvation is indeed a free gift of God, but the kingdom will cost you your life. However, it also gains true life for you.

Now let's go back to that "rest" we were talking about. How do you find it and how do you stay there? Can you truly enter rest?

> *"And he stayed two full years in his own rented quarters and was welcoming all who came to him, preaching the kingdom of God and teaching concerning the Lord Jesus Christ with all openness, unhindered."*
> Acts 28:30

Paul has always been a personal hero of mine. He preached the kingdom with power. This last verse of Acts gives insight into his ministry and his message. What you read in the epistles is all about being a kingdom Christian. In those letters, he preached Christ crucified and the cross. (I Corinthians) He said he had laid a foundation and it was up to everyone else about how they would build on it. (I Corinthians 3:10-15) When he spoke of the message of the cross he said;

> *"For the word of the cross is foolishness to those who are perishing, but to us who are being saved it is the power of God."*
> 1 Corinthians 1:18

Chapter 9

The power I have been speaking about lies just on the other side of the cross. Remember the message Paul gave in chapter 6 of Romans? He said that in water baptism, we follow the path that Jesus took through His death, burial, and resurrection. Jesus asked those disciples who were looking for recognition if they could have the baptism He was about to have–speaking of His coming crucifixion. (Mark 10:38-39). In water baptism, we symbolically follow the path of Jesus, but are in reality to walk that walk in our lives and in a certain sense, experience that same death. Not the pain and suffering He endured on our behalf of course, but an uncomfortable walk none the less. It is a walk that crucifies the flesh and all its desires and releases the Spirit into our lives in all its power. It is a walk leading to rest. You must take it and go through the cross. You must get thorough the cross to experience the resurrection power.

Here is the walk I am talking about. Jesus, during the week prior to His crucifixion, went through many experiences which are very relatable to the experiences you will face if you decide to walk the faith walk of a kingdom minded believer. He came into Jerusalem and experienced the reception of acceptance and acclaim. He entered the temple; despising the sin He saw and threw out those who would make it a place of carnality. His enemies laid trap after trap for Him, that they might find a reason to accuse Him and discredit Him. He went to the upper room and shared the Passover with those He loved, giving them the example of servanthood as He washed their feet. Then he went with a few to the Garden of Gethsemane and agonized in prayer over the trial that loomed ahead. There He surrendered His will to the will of His Father. He was betrayed by someone most close to Him. Then He gave himself to those who would abuse Him, not trying to argue His case, but surrendering to the death that lay ahead. Those He loved deserted Him. He carried the means of His own death, though He was given help along the way. He allowed Himself to be nailed to the cross and crucified, forgiving His detractors and surrendering His soul to His Father, though moments before He had felt forsaken by His Father. He died, was buried, and rose again on the third day, never to experience death again, but only the power that raised Him from the dead.

So how does that all apply to you? I see these experiences as common to a kingdom walk. They come toward the end of your proving times. After you have moved in Christianity for a while and learned a little of the word of God and begin to have a relational experience with Jesus, you will come to this part of your Christian experience if you are willing to go there.

When you first determine to accomplish the vision of God that lies ahead of you, you will find great acceptance from those around you, even acclaim from some. It will feel good and you will be tempted to stay here. Trust me, it's not real and you will need to get through the acceptance and acclaim and enter the city. You go forward from there to the temple.

Paul said to the Corinthians, "Do you not know that you are a temple of God and that the Spirit of God dwells in you?" (1 Corinthians 3:16) On the way to 'rest' as a kingdom Christian, you will be called upon to get rid of sin in your life and make your 'temple' a holy house of prayer. You will need to chase those things out of your life that are sucking the life of the spirit right out of you. You will need to cleanse your temple. This is but the beginning.

Once you have done that, the enemy will lay trap after trap for you to try to discredit you and cause you to defile the temple once again. You will be tempted in many ways to fall, and if you give in to the temptation and move into the sin, you will not be able to complete what lies ahead. You can not walk in the flesh and in the spirit at the same time. You will have to make those 'hard' choices here, choices for what lies ahead and not what is held in the moment. Since you will have come to know what lies ahead without naiveté, there will be great temptation to indulge your flesh. Resist it.

Chapter 9

There comes a point in your vision where you have a tendency to relate everything and everyone around you in reference to how they relate to your vision. You will be tempted to see those around you as people that can help you fulfill your vision. While this is intrinsically accurate, and those around you inevitably could be used by God to help you fulfill your vision, this is not their value or their ultimate purpose. You have come to the "feet washing" moment. You will need to surrender to becoming everyone else's servant and trust God to fulfill your vision as you serve everyone else. You will need to stop seeing those around you through your vision and begin to see them through the vision God has for them. If you don't, you will meet with great resistance going forward until you do. It is the one who humbles himself who is exalted. (James 4:10) This is not so hard if you are willing to give up the glory of success as you might define it and 'fail' in everyone else's eyes.

The next part of your kingdom experience that parallels Jesus' last week is the Gethsemane experience. There is a time you will see the death of yourself looming ahead and you will cry out in your Garden of Gethsemane, "God, let this cup pass from me." You must say the second part of that statement to gain the kingdom: "Yet not my will but Your will be done." The outcome must remain in His hands and you must be surrendered to it. This place in your experience is not a time for action, but a time for prayer. It is a time to prepare for death, the death of your own self-will. Your will must die, that His will might be fulfilled in you.

Somewhere along your path to serve God as He called you to serve Him, you will experience the betrayal of someone whom you have trusted and brought close to you. I know of no instance that someone who moved forward in God's purpose didn't experience this at sometime in their pursuit of the kingdom. Perhaps this experience is necessary so you can have the testimony that John gave about Jesus.

> *"Now when He was in Jerusalem at the Passover, during the feast, many believed in His name, observing His signs which He was doing. But Jesus, on His part, was not entrusting Himself to them, for He knew all men, and because He did not need anyone to testify concerning man, for He Himself knew what was in man."*
> John 2:23-25

You are meant to trust God—not men. This doesn't mean you are to walk around paranoid, distrusting everyone in your life. It simply means that you need to know who it is that you can truly trust and not fall apart when someone you thought you could trust betrays you.

In His path to the cross, He had those He lead and served who deserted Him. So will you. This is also part of this parallel path to the power of the resurrection. Many times you will begin to serve those around you. Then you will come upon a "shadow of death" moment in your life. You will look around to those you have served and who you now would like to have serve you, but they will be nowhere to be found. You will feel very much alone. Here is another 'turn around' moment in your life. If you give in to the natural tendency to feel sorry for yourself, you will turn around and look for the wider road. Give up for yourself the imagined right to have the support of those you have served.

Often times, you will indeed carry the cross upon which you will be crucified. Jesus told us that is what being a disciple required. "Whoever does not carry his own cross and come after Me cannot be My disciple." (Luke 14:27-28) If God has called you to begin some kingdom business or community service for the kingdom, or to just serve in a local church, many times it will become your cross and you will bear the burden of it on your shoulders. While it is possible that some Simon of Cyrene may come to help you on the road to Golgotha, mostly you will carry your own cross. Is a disciple above his teacher or a slave above his master? Of course not. You will have to experience the "fellowship of His suffering" in order to experience the "power of His resurrection." When you look around for those you thought you could count on for support and they are missing, do not fall victim to accusing God. It is not God who deserted you, but those you were meant to serve, not benefit from. As you serve others, the thought that they should serve you in return becomes very strong. It is a lie. Don't fall for it.

In the end, you will have to look around you and surrender yourself to whatever outcome the Father has determined. You will not be able to require anything in the outcome except that His will be done. Many times you will think you know the will of God, only to find out there was a whole lot more that you didn't see than you did see. This is not evidence of an inability to hear, but that God simply doesn't show you all things before He brings them to pass. This, too, is meant to increase your faith. It is a blessing when He gives us the opportunity to simply place our trust in Him.

God will ask you a question. One to which you must always be able to answer "yes". That question is, "Do you trust me?" Do you trust me when your world is falling apart? Do you trust me when you lose something near and dear to you? Do you trust me when everyone else stops trusting me? Do you trust me when your eyes, ears, all of you, can see no hope? It is when you can truly say "yes" to those questions at those times, that you begin to enter the 'rest' that is found in the kingdom of God.

Thus says the LORD, "Cursed is the man who trusts in mankind and makes flesh his strength, and whose heart turns away from the LORD. For he will be like a bush in the desert and will not see when prosperity comes, but will live in stony wastes in the wilderness, a land of salt without inhabitant. "Blessed is the man who trusts in the LORD and whose trust is the LORD. For he will be like a tree planted by the water, that extends its roots by a stream and will not fear when the heat comes; but its leaves will be green, and it will not be anxious in a year of drought nor cease to yield fruit."
Jeremiah 17:5-8

Chapter 10
Kingdom Economics 101

"For where your treasure is, there your heart will be also."
Luke 12:34

British economist Lionel Robbins defines economics as: "the science which studies human behavior as a relationship between ends and scarce means which have alternative uses." The principle of scarcity states that human wants and needs exceed production possibilities and limited resources. When you consider kingdom economics you must realize it is completely different from world economics, since scarcity is not an issue for God. The whole concept of world economics is built upon limited supply and decisions based upon obtaining that supply. In contrast, kingdom economics are built upon unlimited supply and divine distribution built on principles of stewardship. Supply is obtained simply by remaining committed to the source and accepting His will for it. For the sake of this chapter I will relate to the economics of the kingdom of darkness as "world economics" and when I am referring to the economics of God's kingdom I will refer to it simply as kingdom economics.

You have to realize that in the kingdom of darkness, value is not based upon true value, but rather perceived value. For example, a few decades ago in 1975, a small smooth rock of no special note was worth $3.95. That's comparable to roughly $10 in today's currency. In reality it had no real value. Though I suppose it could be used as a paper weight, other than that, it was worthless. The world's economic law of supply and demand set the value at $3.95, and stores couldn't get packaged rocks fast enough to meet the demand. On top of that, a service industry developed around the product. It became possible to send the rock on vacations or for therapy or psychoanalysis, for prices based upon desire, obviously not value. Pet rocks garnered a service industry long before Cabbage Patch dolls did the same thing.

Chapter 10

The pet rock phenomenon is just one example of when the economics of the world demonstrate a lack of consistency in the relationship of value to cost. Throughout the world, needs are defined more by desire than reality. The richer the country, the more likely the worthless is to have greater value. For example, in the U.S. the sports and entertainment industries are paid well beyond their worth if one compares salaries to a real value model.

In world economics, the law of supply and demand is key. This economic law is tied to desire. If one can create sufficient desire, then demand dictates a value higher than the worth of the object. If one can increase the buying power of a culture, and then increase the desire for products, a lifestyle can develop which moves price well beyond value for many things. In the U.S., two-income families have become the norm because indulgent lifestyles have been built upon two incomes and the desire for those material things created by mass media. TV advertising shouts incessantly that you deserve and need more. After you carry this two-income concept through several generations, it seems almost slothful not to function in the established norm. However, since increased income also creates increased desire, prices rise and purchasing power drops. In reality, today's two-income family in the U.S. really doesn't have much more buying power than last century's one-income family.

The engines which drive the world's economics are basic greed and fear. Because the world economy functions on a limited supply basis, the energy required to maintain a larger than average portion of that supply is much greater. Because scarcity is inherent in its principles, fear becomes the decision maker for most people. And, since it is the nature of man to look on the outward appearance and the world mentality creates a strong desire to obtain the respect and admiration of one's peers, the motivation to pursue outward gains will be great. Therefore, many are willing to give up the truly valuable things in life in order to obtain the baser or less valuable things. Sacrifices are made which, considered in the light of the kingdom, make little or no sense, though in the minds of the world they make perfect sense. Family time is traded for overtime. Having the mother present during a child's formative years is traded for a second income. Rather than raising children in the nurture and admonition of the Lord, parents send them to daycare and their children are raised by strangers who have no real concern for their outcome. Job and status takes precedence over the joys of relationship with the kids. Since so much effort is put toward bringing in greater income, simpler lifestyles are traded for the more extravagant, a reward for the energy expended while neglecting the family and working more. That logic defies wisdom.

This is not the only way the prince of darkness defrauds his citizens. Additionally, there is planned obsolescence, inflation created by greed (television has been most helpful in feeding this area), increasing the availability of debt and introducing the use of credit cards so the debt to asset ratio becomes extremely skewed. This in turn has caused more people to enter into debt slavery. The world economy encouraged two-income families by creating a social acceptance of career over homemaking for women, especially in the United States. To a great degree, the two-income family was also fueled by the need to deal with the increase in debt-based purchasing. Because a family can increase their debt load unencumbered by much oversight, they quickly overextend their debt to asset ratio, demanding they generate more income to pay for their interest encumbered purchases. Since many credit purchases are either sustenance based or frivolous, therefore having no intrinsic value, there are no assets available for sale to relieve debt. The Proverbs statement "The borrower is servant to the lender" has developed real definition in our culture at this end of the age. I have addressed this topic more as comparison and to help you realize the transformation you will need in your thinking to enter kingdom economics than as an in depth study. When you look at the world closely, it can be quite sobering.

However, be of good cheer. Christ has overcome the world. Enter the concept of kingdom economics. As for many of the "laws" or principals the world functions under, in Christ you can function under entirely different principles—or not. That choice is up to you. The Son truly does set you free, free to function in any mode you choose. The choice is something which requires a conscious decision. The key, as in everything else kingdom related, is to place this part of your life under the spiritual laws of the kingdom of light rather than the kingdom of darkness. The way to do this is to surrender to the lordship of the King of Kings and give up your control. There are a few principles you must adhere to in this process.

Principle One:

Come to the realization that all of your previous worldly thinking has to undergo a radical transformation.

Paul wrote the following to the Christians in Rome: "And do not be conformed to this world, but be transformed by the renewing of your mind, so that you may prove what the will of God is, that which is good and acceptable and perfect." (Romans 12:3) I understand this applies to much of Christianity, but when you set out to become kingdom minded in finances, it becomes even more imperative. This is particularly true within the United States because of its wealth and lifestyle. This country is one of the most extravagant consumers of the world's resources, and has developed an economic philosophy that is less associated to the reality of value than in many other areas of the world.

Principle Two:
Realize there is no shortage!

So why, you ask, do you have to do without? The answer is simple. Either you were functioning under world economics, or you really didn't do without. Maybe you were lacking against the standards of the world, though you really didn't lack against the standards of life. James gives more definition to this in his letter: "You lust and do not have; so you commit murder. You are envious and cannot obtain; so you fight and quarrel. You do not have because you do not ask. You ask and do not receive, because you ask with wrong motives, so that you may spend it on your pleasures." (James 4:2-3) These two verses I think give a good understanding of the emotions prevalent in our thinking about economic needs versus wants. Very often the world defines wants as needs, and then blames God for not providing them. Similarly, world economics encourages using credit for non asset-related purchases, leaving people stuck trying to relieve the financial pressure God had no intention for them to experience in the first place.

The other scenario James addresses is that God simply has not been included in the process. World economics are followed instead, either through lack of willingness or simply out of ignorance. If you finish this chapter, you will no longer function in ignorance, though some may choose to willfully function outside of God's economic plan, unwilling to submit to God's authority in their finances. Too many refuse God's authority to direct their lives. When you refuse God and retain control, you are only left with what you can do, and not what God can do. This really doesn't empower you in your finances, since your inability to see the future renders you totally blind to what lies ahead.

So where does the idea that there is no shortage in kingdom economics come from? Read the following verses.

> *"The earth is the LORD'S, and all it contains, The world, and those who dwell in it." Psalms 24:1*

Chapter 10

"For every beast of the forest is Mine, The cattle on a thousand hills. "I know every bird of the mountains, And everything that moves in the field is Mine. "If I were hungry I would not tell you, For the world is Mine, and all it contains."
Psalms 50:10-12

"The silver is Mine and the gold is Mine,' declares the LORD of hosts."
Haggai 2:8

"For the LORD your God is bringing you into a good land, a land of brooks of water, of fountains and springs, flowing forth in valleys and hills; a land of wheat and barley, of vines and fig trees and pomegranates, a land of olive oil and honey; a land where you will eat food without scarcity, in which you will not lack anything; a land whose stones are iron, and out of whose hills you can dig copper. When you have eaten and are satisfied, you shall bless the LORD your God for the good land which He has given you."
Deuteronomy 8:7-10

From these scriptures there can be little doubt everything created and all wealth in the world is at God's disposal. Therefore in His economics, there is no shortage. He even promised the nation of Israel there would be no shortage when they entered into their promised land. In allegory, our promised land carries the same assurance and part of the promise of entering God's rest is definitely encompassed in kingdom economics. (See Hebrews 3:12—4:11)

Imagine, if you will, that you are living a life where you never have to wonder how you are going to pay your bills or cover your debts. Imagine a life where you never have to fret about the coming day. Can you imagine it? You wouldn't need to worry about what you were going to eat or what you would put on or...wait—isn't that something like what Jesus talked about once? Interestingly enough, it is associated with the pursuit of the kingdom.

> *"Do not worry then, saying, 'What will we eat?' or 'What will we drink?' or 'What will we wear for clothing?'" "For the Gentiles eagerly seek all these things; for your heavenly Father knows that you need all these things. "But seek first His kingdom and His righteousness, and all these things will be added to you."*
> Matthew 6:31-33

So then why is this lifestyle so hard to imagine? Because few Christians are involved in kingdom economics. Most are functioning completely or mostly in the economics of this world. Their thinking and practices in life and finances are consistently governed by the world system of scarcity-based economics. Perceived self worth is defined by their ability to function within the world's set of financial principles.

Please be aware. I am not promoting a prosperity doctrine. The concept of God showering you with earthly indulgences as some token of His affection for you is to me a very immature and limited understanding of who God is and the role you have in the kingdom. Yes! Many times He may choose to bless you with 'things' Yes! He may cause your life to be materially blessed. Mostly however, what we have is ours so we can use it to bless others and not just ourselves. If we would take the time to check with God and see what He wants done with it, He would cause us to prosper in all aspects and not just earthly treasures.

Chapter 10

Principle three:

Exchange world currency for kingdom currency through tithing.

So how does one practically exchange world economics for kingdom economics? Remember I said this would require a conscious choice on your part? You must decide to present your increase to the Lord so He can exchange the world currency you function under for the currency of the kingdom. This is accomplished through tithing. It is the first step in submitting your wealth to the kingdom. Tithing is a sort of where the rubber hits the road act of obedience that will open the door to kingdom economics. The reason this is so primary is that tithing is how your heart will be planted in the kingdom, because "Where your treasure is your heart will be also."

One way I can immediately spot someone who has less spiritual maturity is to watch how they relate to tithing. You see, tithing has little to do with money, and much to do with submitting your finances to God. I suppose the Church is partly to blame, because it often does a less than stellar job at dealing with the subject, very often making money and the supply of money a central issue. Since supply is not an issue in kingdom economics, for a pastor or evangelist or any other church leader to relate to their needs or the needs of the church and tithing in the same breath is a travesty. If there is a shortage, it has less to do with scarcity than with being out of God's plan. Many times I have watched God purposely dry up finances, either to get a pastor's attention or simply to prevent a church from becoming something He hadn't planned for it to become yet. Sometimes a few years down the road, He releases the necessary income and growth, only to have the church leaders pat themselves on the back for their great evangelism program or some other such program to which they attributed their growth. Most pastors I know who are functioning as kingdom pastors have little idea why the church they served as a pastor suddenly grew. By the same token, a small church with limited income is not necessarily evidence of an inept pastor or staff.

Though a church gets its revenue from tithing, tithing is not the source of money for a local church any more than your job is the source of income for you. I understand this concept can be hard to grasp, but you must grasp it in order to enter kingdom economics. God is, was, and ever shall be the source of all your needs whether a pastor leading a church with financial shortages, a person struggling with debt, or a business facing a cash flow shortage and in need of revenue to survive.

I remember when my wife first came to grips with this principle. She had begun to look at me as the provider for the home. Sure, I was the channel God used to provide for our family many times, but my role was no more key than hers, which was minding the stewardship of the funds God provided through me. I believe God purposely sent us through lean times to bring this realization home to her. I lost a job because of cut backs in a company I worked for. Before I left however, the company offered me a lesser paying position which I simply couldn't afford to take. I had a commute of three plus hours a day, which made sense when I was earning enough to pay for my gas and wear and tear on my vehicle. The job required I use my own vehicle, so ride share or public transportation was not an option available to me. Since the wage they offered for the second position was only a little over half the wage of my original position, I had little choice but to decline. Since they had offered me a job however, Unemployment refused to compensate me for the time I would need to find another job. We went from having a decent income to having no income. Fortunately, God had told us to clear our debts some time before that, but we still had the normal housing and living needs. The church where I served as an elder helped us out considerably during this time, and though the time was pretty humbling, we always had a roof over our head and three meals (though not always square). Mostly the power was on, and since we live in Southern California where it seldom gets very cold, we never froze. Since we live in the Mojave desert, it sometimes does get a bit nippy in the winter, but we had a wood burning stove in one of our rooms and we would spend most of our time there, where we would burn scrap wood to stay warm.

We went for well over a year in this period of shortage. I would find small jobs which brought in a meager amount. I often got less than the prevailing wage because I would lower my bid in order to obtain the work. This brought in a little income, not enough to remove the pressure but enough to survive. All other efforts to obtain income, build any sort of business, or obtain employment failed. During this period, my wife become very unsettled and would often query me, "What are you going to do!?" Since I was doing all I could to try to solve the problem my answer was always the same. "I will continue to seek the Lord for the answer." This was delivered with varying degrees of impatience. It was a less than satisfactory reply for her, and by her responses, I could see that in many ways she was looking at me as her provider who she could no longer count on. Once when I pointed this out—in less than a spiritual manner, during a time of rather heated emotions—the light turned on for her. We stopped arguing about our circumstances and sought the Lord together for our situation. When she became concerned, she would remind herself that she was to look not at me as the source, but turn fully to God for her needs. Oh, she would keep me informed so I could pray too, and we spent much time in prayer together. It changed things for us, and definitely for her. She realized God would provide for her alone and she was not dependent on me for her needs. After a little over a year, God restored our circumstances and we moved into less stressful times. The point I am making: stop looking at your usual source of income as your provision, and look toward God. Do not make your business, your job, or your spouse's job your God.

The Lord has provided something called tithing as a method of making Him Lord over your finances in action. Sadly, I have seen some Christians loudly proclaim they have been set free from tithing. They are under grace, they say, not under the law, and they forcefully proclaim that tithing is no longer relevant to them. Too bad, since tithing is such a benefit to the many who live by it. Their proclamations show that their understanding of tithing is incomplete. It is true—we are free in Christ and are not under the law. However, though tithing was clearly defined in the Law of Moses, it predates law, and is a principle which has been around as long as the concept of sacrificial death for sin. You are truly free to not tithe, but you are also free to tithe, and thus walk in the benefit this kingdom provision gives. You are also free to live in sin and not avail yourself of the benefits of the death Jesus died on the cross for you, but the alternate outcome makes the choice sort of a moot point. From what I read in the Bible, the alternate to tithing is also a moot point.

First the word itself. The word in the Hebrew is ma`aser (mah-as-ayr'); a tenth. In the Greek it is dekatoo (dek-at-o'-o); "to give or take a tenth". (This is the origin of the word "decade".) The word defines its own value, and in the Mosaic Law it was defined as the "first" tenth. The word "tithe" quantifies what is being talked about. It is a tenth. It is not 20% or 5% but 10%. Anything over a tithe is better defined as "offerings". You can give as much as you want, but your "tithe" is 10% of your increase. Words have meaning. If I say I am giving a 15% tithe, I am misusing the term. If I throw $10 in the offering plate from a high four figure monthly income, I haven't tithed, unless I just received $100 as a gift and was giving God the first tenth or the "tithe". The reason I am being so definitive on this is that it is this "tenth" which activates the economic laws of the kingdom of light for your money and moves your currency into a new value system. Tithing is a different principle in the kingdom than "giving", which is an add-on benefit expanded on in the New Covenant of the kingdom.

Tithe is based upon your increase. Increase is defined as anything which becomes yours to use—whether to pay taxes with or pay your bills or just use as you want. In other words—your gross income. If someone gives you a gift of money, it is increase and the Bible tells us the first 10% belongs to the Lord. It is a "tithe" and holy to the Lord. 5% is not a tithe any more than 5% is 10%. I like to consider it the exchange rate for kingdom currency. When I receive money from any source I can do whatever is needed or wanted with it. I have a full range of choices. Some can be bad choices and some good. For example, when I go to South Africa, I immediately exchange my U.S. currency for the South African Rand. I don't have to, mind you. It is not required by law. If I wanted, I could go out on the streets of Johannesburg and purchase whatever I wanted or needed with my American money. However, it wouldn't buy near as much. Street exchange for our currency is much less than the official exchange rates. By using an established currency exchange center, I am then able to turn my American money into South African money and go out to the markets and buy much more with their rand than I would have with my U.S. dollar. Though I do have to pay a fee for the exchange, I end up with more buying power even though I have to give up a portion of it for the exchange. I am using this allegorically with kingdom principles. Tithing becomes the way to exchange your world currency with kingdom currency which will make your 90% have way more purchasing power than if you had retained 100% of your world currency.

God explains this in Malachi.

> *"Bring the whole tithe into the storehouse, so that there may be food in My house, and test Me now in this," says the LORD of hosts, "if I will not open for you the windows of heaven and pour out for you a blessing until it overflows. Then I will rebuke the devourer for you, so that it will not destroy the fruits of the ground; nor will your vine in the field cast its grapes," says the LORD of hosts. All the nations will call you blessed, for you shall be a delightful land," says the LORD of hosts."*
> Malachi 3:10-12

This passage is very revealing in that it defines the kingdom effects associated with this principle of tithing. The basis of world economics is scarcity. Add to this the concept of planned obsolescence and built in depreciation making regular replacement a normal part of life, keeping ones head above water becomes problematical. However, if I enter into kingdom economics I can enjoy the benefits which that economy brings. He promises me He will rebuke the devourer and make my circumstances more beneficial. My cars don't break down as often. My clothes last longer. I am able to obtain better deals and spend less money. God in turn will bring opportunities my way which otherwise couldn't have been mine. By exchanging my world currency for kingdom currency, I now have what God can do with my income as opposed to what only I would be able to do with it. Trust me on this! He is a way better financial planner than you are. Way better than Merrill Lynch even. (Yes, I'm being facetious.)

I would also like to add one thing here. Those who are proponents of not tithing lay claim to the fact that it is never addressed in the epistles. To that I would reply: you build doctrine from what the Bible says and not from what it doesn't say. There are many topics that are left untouched in the epistles but covered in great detail elsewhere. It is from the "elsewhere" that you must draw your doctrine and not from the "unmentioned-in-some-parts."

This passage in Malachi also defines some of the concepts about tithing. For example, the tithe goes into the local storehouse. Your local storehouse on a personal level is your church. It is the place where you get fed spiritually and where the tithe is taken. It is also a place where you don't decide what happens to it. It gets it out of your hands and into the hands of the Lord. "Wait!" you say. "Men are deciding what to do with this money." That is true, and they will indeed give an account to God with what they do with it. God is able to guard His money without your help. If you are in the church God placed you, then He will oversee the handling or mishandling of His money. "It's a terrible thing to fall into the hands of the living God." (Hebrews 10:31) If His tithe is mishandled He will take care of it.

If you don't have a local church, then seek one until you do. To not be submitted to a local church family is definitely out of the will of God as defined in the Bible. If you have left your home church because God moved you, then continue to tithe where you were until He places you in a new local church. If you discovered He hadn't really placed you in that body and you were premature in settling there, then give your tithe where He tells you until you have established where your church family is going to be.

Business tithing is another aspect. The Lord may tell a business owner to tithe on their business revenue. Since it does not fall under the same concepts as an individual in reference to the local storehouse, the tithe goes to wherever the Lord tells your organization to give it. Do what He tells you to do with it. One thing I do know; tithe belongs to Him and needs to go outside of your decision-making control in order to be considered a 'tithe". If you are a business owner, ask God what kingdom organization He wants you to fund with your tithe and give it to that organization. Do not create an organization to use your own tithe. The principle of tithing is surrender, surrender of control and power to the Lord. My church gives a tithe of all of its revenue to other mission organizations which we know are kingdom-minded. We do this so that what remains can accomplish more than if we didn't. There is biblical precedent for a church tithing: "Then the LORD spoke to Moses, saying, "Moreover, you shall speak to the Levites and say to them, 'When you take from the sons of Israel the tithe which I have given you from them for your inheritance, then you shall present an offering from it to the LORD, a tithe of the tithe." (Numbers 18:25-26) There is no such strongly defined biblical precedent for businesses, though I have seen the Lord bless businesses that do apply tithing as a business principle, so I can only assume the principle is universal in kingdom economics. If you run a business, be obedient to the Lord and run it as a kingdom organization. Let Him call the shots and seek His face continually for His plan. God knows way more than you do, and will make your paths sure. Don't do it as legalism, but as obedience, and seek Him for how He wants your company to do it.

I consider the concept of tithing so important, I won't pass a plate at our church except in special circumstances when we are taking a love offering for someone. We teach tithing and put a tithe box in the back. I refuse to give people opportunity to throw some $10 or $20 guilt offering in a plate and thus salve their conscience enough to cause them to forfeit their benefit of tithing. I also will not ever teach tithing and associate it with a specific need within the church. If our church has a need, it is to God we must turn, the same as you as an individual. While I think it is important that those who call this church their church home know what's happening, I will give out that information at our prayer gathering, not our regular service, so that the solution can be sought at the same time the difficulty is announced. God is our source of revenue and though He uses the tithe to handle it, the tithe is His and is not the solution. He is!

Chapter 10

Principle four:
When you sow in another man's field, you will reap in your own. It is the principle of giving. As in most principles of the kingdom, it will function best when used in conjunction with the leading of the Holy Spirit.

I have seen this work in many circumstances. You take what resources you have and apply them to help another. Later you find that your resources have been multiplied further down the road. The apostle I grew up under and consider to be my spiritual father in the faith would say to us elders whenever the church was having lean times, "The church seems to be having financial difficulty. Is there someone we can give money to, directed by the will of God?" We then would help an individual or another church out, and our pressures would get resolved. In my own church, any time I have ministered in Africa, I would come back and see God give our church a spiritual deposit or growth.

> *"Give and it will be given to you. They will pour into your lap a good measure—pressed down, shaken together, and running over. For by your standard of measure it will be measured to you in return."*
> Luke 6:38

> *"Now this I say, he who sows sparingly will also reap sparingly, and he who sows bountifully will also reap bountifully. Each one must do just as he has purposed in his heart, not grudgingly or under compulsion, for God loves a cheerful giver. And God is able to make all grace abound to you, so that always having all sufficiency in everything, you may have an abundance for every good deed."*
> 2 Corinthians 9:6-9

I call this the principle of giving. It functions in addition to and outside of the principle of tithing. It transcends earthly goods and relates value to value. Whatever you sow in your neighbor's field, you will reap in your own. Ecclesiastes says, "Cast your bread on the surface of the waters, for you will find it after many days."

When obedient in the kingdom economic principles given here—and please be assured this is not a definitive list—and declaring the first tenth of your gross as holy to the Lord and giving it to your local storehouse which is your church family, your currency becomes kingdom currency. What now?

A couple of points you need to implement. Since there is no scarcity in God's kingdom, a lack is an indication to seek the Lord to discover His will. James said "You have not because you don't ask." So of course, make your request known to the Lord. Then you wait. You don't implement some creative financing—unless of course He tells you to. You wait until He parts the Red Sea. God many times uses provision, or lack thereof, to cause a change of course. I established a kingdom business in Southern California. It required a fairly large amount of capital to begin, and though I had only raised about $40,000 for it over a couple of months, I felt the Lord told me to go ahead. Equipped with what I considered a mandate from the Lord, I began to make the needed plans to establish the business. It was an Internet Service Provider (ISP) which offered filtered Internet access. Right after I began, another individual contacted me and asked me to help him establish the business in the San Diego area. With our combined efforts, I had a little more money to proceed.

I contacted various resources and set about to establish the business. Everything seemed to be in place when I received a call from one of my two sources of backbone connectivity, telling me they would not be able to fulfill their commitment to provide the service I required. This connection was for 40% of the territory, and left me in a bit of a problem, as it also was for the man who had joined with me from San Diego. I had searched rather diligently for this resource, and this and the one other which was providing connectivity for the rest of my territory were the only available resources I could find. I remembered thinking, "Well its Friday. God can solve it this weekend", and I went home. On Monday morning, before I really had time to find out how God was going to solve the problem, the other provider called and told me they also couldn't deliver. Now everything I had spent the last four weeks arranging was wiped away. Since I had made various commitments against these resources and I had definitive time constraints, the situation was most uncomfortable. I went into my office, closed my door and shades and began to pray. It's amazing how fervently one can pray in seemingly hopeless situations. I emerged from my office a few hours later finally having accepted that if this was a kingdom business and He was God, that if He wanted the whole thing to go up in smoke, that was His business and I was sure He would come up with some way for me to pay off my investors.

Two hours later an individual returned a call I had given them three weeks earlier with not only a solution to all of my problems, but also an efficient and cost effective way to multiply the scope of what I was doing. Within three days from that moment, God had put over $235,000 into my hands and expanded my territory from 3 million to 25 million people. I always laugh when I think about this. It was if God said, "That's cute John. Nice work, but let me show you what I have in mind," and then swept His arm across the table, clearing it of my efforts and laying out His plans.

He is so much more capable than you are. If you will submit your money and your plans together with your self to Him, He will accomplish much with what you could only accomplish little. You have a choice. Give Him every part of your finances, submit yourself to the kingdom and see what He will do, or hang on to your money and see what you can do. To me, it's a no-brainer.

"So all the peoples of the earth will see that you are called by the name of the LORD, and they will be afraid of you. "The LORD will make you abound in prosperity, in the offspring of your body and in the offspring of your beast and in the produce of your ground, in the land which the LORD swore to your fathers to give you. "The LORD will open for you His good storehouse, the heavens, to give rain to your land in its season and to bless all the work of your hand; and you shall lend to many nations, but you shall not borrow. "The LORD will make you the head and not the tail , and you only will be above, and you will not be underneath, if you listen to the commandments of the LORD your God, which I charge you today, to observe them carefully,"
Deuteronomy 28:10-14

CHAPTER 11

What the Kingdom of God is Like

"And He said, "How shall we picture the kingdom of God, or by what parable shall we present it."
Mark 4:30-31

Jesus spent much time in His ministry explaining the nature of the kingdom of God. In Matthew alone, Jesus gave thirty-seven separate instructions concerning the kingdom of God. There are two of the beatitudes which deal with the kingdom, twelve "The kingdom of God is like" parables, and twenty-three other separate instructions about the kingdom. I find it perplexing that the Church has managed to neglect this message as much as it has, considering the emphasis which Jesus put on it. The problem as I see it is that most relegate this message to the afterlife, though Jesus never spoke in a way which indicated He was thinking of the kingdom only in reference to what will come when He returns.

In this chapter I will focus on the "kingdom of heaven is like" parables which Jesus gave us for our understanding of the nature of the kingdom. Since this book is about the kingdom in this age, I will forgo in this book a lengthy explanation of the last four parables. I will address them in another book called The Millennium.

The first two parables require little interpretation, as they are explained for us. When you look at these, pay close attention to the explanation Jesus gives later about the types and symbols he uses in them, as you will need to bring those forward into some of the remaining parables to get an understanding that is biblically accurate.

Chapter 11

1. Parable of the Sower

Parable:

> *"And He spoke many things to them in parables, saying, 'Behold, the sower went out to sow; and as he sowed, some seeds fell beside the road, and the birds came and ate them up. Others fell on the rocky places, where they did not have much soil; and immediately they sprang up, because they had no depth of soil. But when the sun had risen, they were scorched; and because they had no root, they withered away. Others fell among the thorns, and the thorns came up and choked them out. And others fell on the good soil and yielded a crop, some a hundredfold, some sixty, and some thirty. He who has ears, let him hear.'"*
> *Matthew 13:3-9*

This is the only kingdom parable that Christ doesn't begin with a statement telling you He is comparing something natural to the kingdom of God. However, in the explanation which He gives his disciples later, Christ defines the seed as the message of the kingdom. It is interesting to note that before Christ begins to explain this parable to his disciples, he tells them it was given to them, not to just anyone, to understand the message of the kingdom. Discipleship and the kingdom messages are part and parcel of one another.

> *"And the disciples came and said to Him, 'Why do you speak to them in parables?' Jesus answered them, 'to you it has been granted to know the mysteries of the kingdom of heaven, but to them it has not been granted.'"*
> *Matthew 13:10-12*

Here is Christ's explanation of the parable of the sower:

> *"Hear then the parable of the sower. When anyone hears the word of the kingdom and does not understand it, the evil one comes and snatches away what has been sown in his heart. This is the one on whom seed was sown beside the road. The one on whom seed was sown on the rocky places, this is the man who hears the word and immediately receives it with joy; yet he has no firm root in himself, but is only temporary, and when affliction or persecution arises because of the word, immediately he falls away. And the one on whom seed was sown among the thorns, this is the man who hears the word, and the worry of the world and the deceitfulness of wealth choke the word, and it becomes unfruitful.*
> *And the one on whom seed was sown on the good soil, this is the man who hears the word and understands it; who indeed bears fruit and brings forth, some a hundredfold, some sixty, and some thirty."*
> Matthew 13:18-23

Note the seed is defined as being the "word of the kingdom." I have heard some explain this parable by relating the seed to the broader, all-inclusive "word of God" but such is not the case. Jesus clearly defined it for us, as the word of the kingdom. The phrase "of the kingdom" is a prepositional phrase used as an adjective which defines which "word" he is referring to. There is much in the Bible which relates to the kingdom and much which relates to other things. The "seed" of this parable is the "word" which relates to the kingdom.

This is one of the 'mixture' parables. It presents four possible scenarios for results of hearing the word of the kingdom. Same seed—four different results. Those where mixture is present produce no fruit. Only the seed which falls on ground which is good soil—i.e. pure soil—produces any fruit.

First scenario—birds take it away. This is an important definition because it helps us understand another kingdom parable with birds in it that has no recorded explanation. In this parable Jesus tells us the birds are symbolic of "the evil one". Because they are addressed in the plural form, I assume it also includes the demonic forces he commands; ergo, bird(s) symbolize evil one(s)

Second scenario—the "rocky place" indicates lack of depth. Jesus defines the results and what this lack of commitment produces. This soil loves the idea about benefit, but has little time for the trials. It has no patient endurance, consequently can't stand the heat, and gets out of the kitchen. By the way, this "heat" that comes is referred to as affliction or persecution because of the word of the kingdom. He's still talking about the same "word". This is not the normal struggles of life. That comes next. (A little aside here.) Though this is not part of this parable, I have seen that often times the rocky ground crowd will get offended first so it won't feel like it's their fault when they bail—though I am certain they never think that through to its conclusion, deciding to get offended on purpose.)

Third scenario—Cares of this world and wealth choke out the fruit which could have—yes—should have come but didn't. Of the first three, this soil gets the closest to producing fruit. Our world is very subtle at times, and this mixture can creep in and destroy you without you even noticing that it's happened. One day you wake up and look around and realize that every decision you have been making for some time is about how to make natural life happen. Not once in the past many months have you hung out over the edge of a cliff for the benefit of the kingdom, and experienced the rush of watching the Father slay the giants for you, then pick you off the ledge and set you back to safety. Suddenly—or not so suddenly—your life has become mundane and common place, and you are not at all sure what happened to your first love. Thorns–that's what happened. Thorns have deep roots and are very hard to remove from a field. If you've become soil with thorns you need to break up the fallow ground. Maybe it is time to weed. A combination of prayer and fasting is your best bet.

Fourth scenario—the way it's meant to be. Good soil—good seed—good fruit. It's your choice you know—which soil you will end up being. Are you hearing the word of the kingdom? Are you understanding it? If so, then go and produce the fruit of it. God is with you. He'll never leave or forsake you. Sure, you'll have trials. So what? You'll have those whether you produce fruit or not. Why not attach some value to the trials you're going to have anyway? Be honest. If you're one who has not been seeking first the kingdom, but rather the things of this world, how effective have you been in maintaining comfort and security? I bet you have still felt discomfort and experienced rejection. Why not do that for God and produce something eternal like good fruit?

2. Parable of the tares among the wheat

Parable:
> *Jesus presented another parable to them, saying, "The kingdom of heaven may be compared to a man who sowed good seed in his field. But while his men were sleeping, his enemy came and sowed tares among the wheat, and went away. But when the wheat sprouted and bore grain, then the tares became evident also. The slaves of the landowner came and said to him, 'Sir, did you not sow good seed in your field? How then does it have tares?' And he said to them, 'An enemy has done this!' The slaves said to him, 'Do you want us, then, to go and gather them up?' But he said, 'No; for while you are gathering up the tares, you may uproot the wheat with them.*

Chapter 11

Allow both to grow together until the harvest; and in the time of the harvest I will say to the reapers, 'First gather up the tares and bind them in bundles to burn them up; but gather the wheat into my barn.'"
Matthew. 13:24-30

Explanation:
Then He left the crowds and went into the house. And His disciples came to Him and said, "Explain to us the parable of the tares of the field." And He said, "The one who sows the good seed is the Son of Man, and the field is the world; and as for the good seed, these are the sons of the kingdom; and the tares are the sons of the evil one; and the enemy who sowed them is the devil, and the harvest is the end of the age; and the reapers are angels. So just as the tares are gathered up and burned with fire, so shall it be at the end of the age. The Son of Man will send forth His angels, and they will gather out of His kingdom all stumbling blocks, and those who commit lawlessness, and will throw them into the furnace of fire; in that place there will be weeping and gnashing of teeth. Then the righteousness will shine forth as the sun in the kingdom of their Father. He who has ears, let him hear."
Matthew 13:36-43

This is the second parable which Jesus interprets for us. Jesus grew up in an agrarian society, so once again Jesus turns to natural farming issues to define an aspect of the kingdom. This sometime creates difficulty in understanding in a society where most are city dwellers, such as this country. I grew up on a farm and can relate to this parable quite clearly. I will limit my commentary to that which is not self evident, since Jesus pretty well explained this parable. There are a few points I would like to draw your attention to. The evil one is defined here as the devil. He did little work, but his effect was large. He simply sowed tares and left. Tares are plants which appear identical to their fruitful counterparts until it comes time for harvest or during a storm. In a wheat field, the wheat will bend before the wind, while a tare will not. In harvest, the wheat produces so much fruit the weight of it bows the heads of the grain. Not so with the tares which stand proudly tall, becoming very evident as tares. They function on their own and are always semi-destructive, because they suck the nutrients away from everything close to them. If there are enough tares around a good plant, it struggles, since the nutrients which the good plant should receive are sucked up by the users. Tares also drink up the moisture in the soil, making it dry out faster. Because of these things, a farmer takes great care to prepare the soil, getting rid of any roots from last years' tares, and making certain he has good seed. The definition Jesus gives here is that the tares are people who make themselves stumbling blocks within a good field. They are those who don't really accept authority and structure and will never produce fruit. Note this is not rocky soil, not soil covered with thorns, but good soil. It ought to produce good fruit, except the enemy introduces mixture. The tares are there for one reason—to limit the yield of the wheat.

Since Jesus is talking about the kingdom, this is definitely applicable to churches, so pastors please take note. If the tares have gotten a good foothold in your church, follow Jesus' advice and let them grow together with the wheat. They can even serve some benefit, though I would not recommend you let anything depend on them. If you ignore Jesus' advice and try to remove them, you will simply disturb the rest of your flock. (I would add here, you need to distinguish between tares and wolves. Wolves have got to go. Feel free to drive them out.) After this parable, no further explanations to His kingdom parables are recorded. I guess He figured we could get the hang of it after two, because the rest come without an explanation.

Chapter 11

3. Mustard Seed Parable

He presented another parable to them, saying, "The kingdom of heaven is like a mustard seed, which a man took and sowed in his field; and this is smaller than all other seeds, but when it is full grown, it is larger than the garden plants and becomes a tree, so that the birds of the air come and nest in its branches."
Matthew 13:31-32

So let's try our hand at this one without the recorded explanation to fall back on. We have some similar types and symbols here. He again relates to farming and introduces some of the same symbols. He explains, "A man took and sowed in His field". Sounds a lot like kingdom parables one and two doesn't it? And what were the symbolic representations of those parables?

Jesus = the sower
The secular world = the field
The evil one(s), = the devil(s) = bird(s)

You have to go outside the twelve kingdom parables to get an explanation of the symbolism in the mustard seed, but the word of God is faithful and it can be found. This is where a good concordance comes in handy.

And He said to them, "Because of the littleness of your faith; for truly I say to you, if you have faith the size of a mustard seed, you will say to this mountain, 'Move from here to there,' and it will move; and nothing will be impossible to you."
Matthew 17:20-21

So we have the final piece of the puzzle—or parable if you will:
Faith = mustard seed

With the definition of known symbols, greater clarity comes to you when reading this parable. Christ is the author and finisher of your faith. When He plants it in the field of this world, it finds good soil (you) and takes root. There it grows into something which attracts the attention of the enemy who comes and sets up house in its branches. There are a few things to note here. Faith and what it produces is what the kingdom of heaven is like. This parable relates to the information in the last two chapters of this book. Faith is central to growth in the kingdom. A little goes a long way so you don't need much and it will grow into something powerful.

This parable also alerts us to what we can expect if this seed of faith takes root and grows. The enemy will come and infiltrate our efforts. I take this as a prayer alert. It is a warning that if you start a work for the kingdom—like a business, a community ministry or within a church—and it takes root and begins to grow, you need to set up your prayer efforts. If you don't, the birds will be right there to eat all the kingdom seed before it can take root. You must get rid of the birds! This is accomplished on your knees.

4. Leaven Parable

He spoke another parable to them, "The kingdom of heaven is like leaven, which a woman took and hid in three pecks of flour until it was all leavened."
Matthew 13:33

This is another "mixture" parable. Leaven is and always has been the biblical symbol for "sin". The Old Testament and New Testament alike relate to leaven this way. The kingdom of heaven is described as being something where the whole can be changed through the introduction of just a little sin. Christ is not comparing the kingdom to sin but the effects sin has to the whole. This is the outcome of mixture. It permeates the whole, creating something which is totally leavened. It is another strong parable for purity and against mixture or compromise. "Pecks" is probably not the best translation of the Greek word "saton" which is simply a measure without definition; "parts" would be a comparable word in liquid measure. I believe the key word here is "three" not "pecks". This "flour" represents the sons of the kingdom, since the wheat is defined as the sons of the kingdom in the previous parable. Three is the number for the Godhead, of which we are made in the image. (We are created body, soul, and spirit according to I Thessalonians 5:23.) I believe Jesus is telling us here about what hiding sin in a kingdom citizen's life does to his whole being, or for that matter, what allowing sin in a kingdom-minded organization does to the whole organization. Someone who God has used to plant a kingdom project needs to doubly take note here, because one person's sin can affect the whole. It is another parable decrying mixture. It is an alert to what our attitude toward purity needs to be if we are to enter the kingdom.

5. Hidden Treasure Parable

"The kingdom of heaven is like a treasure hidden in the field, which a man found and hid again; and from joy over it he goes and sells all that he has and buys that field."
Matthew 13:44

6. Pearl of Great Price Parable

"Again, the kingdom of heaven is like a merchant seeking fine pearls, and upon finding one pearl of great value, he went and sold all that he had and bought it."
Matthew 13:45-46

These are your two "Kingdom Economics 101" parables. They relate to value vs. cost. I pretty well defined these for you in the last chapter so I won't belabor them again here except to say, let your "all" be all! These are a strong alert to not hang on to anything, but let it all go, so that you might obtain the kingdom.

7. Fishing Net parable

"Again, the kingdom of heaven is like a dragnet cast into the sea, and gathering fish of every kind; and when it was filled, they drew it up on the beach; and they sat down and gathered the good fish into containers, but the bad they threw away. So it will be at the end of the age; the angels will come forth and take out the wicked from among the righteous, and will throw them into the furnace of fire; in that place there will be weeping and gnashing of teeth." Matthew 13:47-50

This is another mixture and harvest parable. It is very similar to the "tares" parable about the kingdom, but much more relatable to the people who made their living from fishing. I believe both of these mixture parables are meant to encourage the good fish and the good wheat. A kingdom Christian will find themselves with many who are not kingdom-minded people, and there will be little difference in the outward appearance. Sometimes you will even find the tares and the bad fish seem to receive better treatment than you. This is an encouragement to not loose heart. God is not fooled, even if some people are. He knows the difference between users and producers even if men don't notice. Nor do you need to prove the tares or the bad fish are bad. The harvest will separate the mixture and the good will receive their reward. If you are just coming into your kingdom citizenship, don't try to sort out who's who. God will sort all that out. Just make certain you decide to be good wheat or good fish. The choice is up to you.

8. Forgiveness parable

"For this reason the kingdom of heaven may be compared to a king who wished to settle accounts with his slaves. When he had begun to settle them, one who owed him ten thousand talents was brought to him. But since he did not have the means to repay, his lord commanded him to be sold, along with his wife and children and all that he had, and repayment to be made. So the slave fell to the ground and prostrated himself before him, saying, 'Have patience with me and I will repay you everything.' And the lord of that slave felt compassion and released him and forgave him the debt. But that slave went out and found one of his fellow slaves who owed him a hundred denarii; and he seized him and began to choke him, saying, 'Pay back what you owe.' So his fellow slave fell to the ground and began to plead with him, saying, 'Have patience with me and I will repay you.' But he was unwilling and went and threw him in prison until he should pay back what was owed. So when his fellow slaves saw what had happened, they were deeply grieved and came and reported to their lord all that had happened. Then summoning him, his lord said to him, 'You wicked slave, I forgave you all that debt because you pleaded with me. Should you not also have had mercy on your fellow slave, in the same way that I had mercy on you?' And his lord, moved with anger, handed him over to the torturers until he should repay all that was owed him. My heavenly Father will also do the same to you, if each of you does not forgive his brother from your heart."
Matthew 18:23-35

I think one of the easiest sins to fall into as you become a kingdom-minded Christian is one of a judgmental attitude. Since you are kingdom, and your reward isn't really in this world and you avoid much of this world's pleasures, it is very easy to begin to feel a superior to those who are still trying to figure out what "good soil" Christianity is. When you are mistreated by them or you are wronged by someone you've served or benefited, it is very easy to fall into the "superior" trap, to forget how much your Father endured from you, and develop a heart of un-forgiveness.

When you are betrayed by someone close to you or deserted by those you had hoped wouldn't desert you, it is easy to begin to feel wounded. When they repent, will you forgive them? This parable tells us that a heart ready to forgive is an essential part of the kingdom. It reminds us to remember from where we came, so we are forgiving to those who need to be forgiven.

The last four parables I believe relate very strongly to the spiritual vs. the natural Israel and how God deals with all of that in the end. I also believe they have much relevance to the Millennium. Because of the complexity of that topic, I will only touch on it in the epilogue and won't comment on these four parables here, but only make a record of them.

I would like to take a few minutes here to talk about eschatology or the study of end times. Since most of those passages which relate to end times are in 'symbol' and 'type' without any convenient recorded explanations by Jesus, it is very definitely open to interpretations which are faulty. I am not dogmatic about much of my eschatology and my thought is this—the end will come and the millennium will begin, and then everyone's end time doctrines will be straightened out. In the meantime, consider the evidence presented and believe what you find biblically convincing. None of it is absolute or imperative to your walk with the Lord. What is imperative is your walk with the Lord. Focus on that.

Chapter 11

Here are the last four kingdom parables which relate to the kingdom in the end times.

9. Vineyard workers Parable

"For the kingdom of heaven is like a landowner who went out early in the morning to hire laborers for his vineyard . . ."
Matthew 20:1-16

10. Wedding feast parable

Jesus spoke to them again in parables, saying, "The kingdom of heaven may be compared to a king who gave a wedding feast for his son . . ."
Matthew 22:1-14

11. Ten wise /foolish virgins

"Then the kingdom of heaven will be comparable to ten virgins, who took their lamps and went out to meet the bridegroom . . ."
Matthew 25:1-13

12. Parable of the Talents

"For it [the kingdom] is just like a man about to go on a journey, who called his own slaves and entrusted his possessions to them . . ."
Matthew 25:14-30

Jesus spoke the truths of His kingdom in parables so that it could only be found by those who would seek it with all their heart. His presentation of the kingdom was that it would require effort to find, and there would be some who wouldn't. He spoke strongly against compromise or mixture. His parables give us an estimation of the value and worth of obtaining the kingdom. They tell us the composition of the kingdom and how the Gentiles were going to be brought in. He speaks of the rewards of entering the kingdom. In the wedding feast parable He tells us many are called but few are chosen. There is distinct separation referenced in regards to what the kingdom is like, and the indication is not between saved and unsaved, but between saved and saved. This message which Jesus preached is not a popular message. It was not well received in His day and is not finding a broad acceptance here in this age. Yet it is the message He wants preached—so let it be preached by those who would preach it.

> *"Have you understood all these things?" They said to Him, "Yes." And Jesus said to them, "Therefore every scribe who has become a disciple of the kingdom of heaven is like a head of a household, who brings out of his treasure things new and old."*
> *Matthew 13:51-52*

CHAPTER 12
Maintaining Your Supply Lines

When involved in military warfare, one of the biggest mistakes a field officer could make was to outdistance his ability to maintain his supply lines. If the enemy made a flank run and cut off his supply, he had only a short time before his trucks no longer ran and his tanks ground to a halt and he was overrun by the enemy. The same thing was true of his communication. His ability to communicate to his commander and his artillery support was essential in order for him to accomplish his purpose. It is quite easy to see the applicability of this metaphor to your Christian experience and to understand why you encounter so much spiritual resistance to maintaining both of these. You must be careful to be in constant contact with your supplier and you also need to know where He is going to expect you to be, if you wish to have provision made for your mission. If you do this, He says you will be fruitful. He is not saying you might be fruitful or you could be fruitful but rather, you will bear fruit.

"If you abide in Me, and My words abide in you, ask whatever you wish, and it will be done for you."
John 15:7

Wow! Now there's a promise! "Ask whatever you wish and it will be done for you." Careful though. Don't miss the qualifier. "If you abide in me and my words abide in you," has to be fulfilled for this scripture to have relevance no matter how worthy you consider your purpose. This is what the kingdom is all about. I know an immature Christian who wished and asked for a Maserati, just to become disappointed when the loan application didn't clear the bank. While that example might seem far-fetched and most Christians realize

Chapter 12

that God is not their magic genie in a bottle, the same qualifier holds true for nobler pursuits. If you are 'abiding' then the will of the father is in you and you are walking by the same parameters our Lord walked, His testimony being, "I only do those things the Father tells me to do."

To be able to live in that level of harmony with the Lord requires a readiness and practice so you can truly say, "His words (rhema) abide in me." There are two Greek words that are translated into the English "word(s)" One is "logos" and the other is "rhema". One is the established, written word, and the other is the proceeding word. Christ says His active, proceeding words must abide in you. He must be speaking to you and you must be listening. That requires a continual connection to the source. What you read today or what He said to you last week needs what He's saying to you today. You can't walk in yesterday's revelation or just the written word and still abide in Him and have His words abiding in you. You must stay connected to the source.

A little about listening; It takes practice. If you have recently been saved, hearing is not going to be particularly precise or all that recognizable. Even after you have been doing it a while, you still question whether or not you are hearing God's voice. When the Spirit speaks in your mind, you hear it in the sound of your own thoughts. It is the content and impact that is different, and after a while it becomes less problematic to discern the difference—unless of course you never practice. There are some helps I use when I get particularly deaf—which happens when I fill my life with too much stuff. I go to the "logos" or written word anywhere in Psalms and begin to read it out loud to myself until I begin to hear the Lord reading it to me. (You must read it out loud for it to be effective. Faith comes by "hearing.") I never get more than a few chapters before the Lord begins to speak. When He reads it, the heartfelt response is much greater. Reading Proverbs is also a good way to prime your spiritual pump, so to speak. The whole point is, you must hear Him and His words must abide in you in order for you to abide in Him. If you become deaf, you must make the effort and take the time to get your hearing back.

One of the most common mistakes I see in the lives of Christians is the innate belief there is sufficient power within themselves to accomplish their purpose and they really don't need to put that much energy into the process of staying connected to the source. I would have to say, the only effort that is essential from you is staying connected to the source. If you do this, you will spend little time spinning your wheels or trying to recover from a misstep. If you become and stay connected you will enter the kingdom of God forcefully, and forcefully lay hold of it because you will be under the direction and authority of your commander and chief. Jesus spent much time telling us what the kingdom of God is like. As you read about all He described the kingdom to be, it is very easy to begin to feel overwhelmed by what is involved in kingdom living. That is because you often think the accomplishment of those requirements rests in the ability of your flesh to perform. Since your flesh has let you down in the past, you have little confidence it will work for you in the present or in the future. Remember it is not up to your flesh to produce fruit that remains. It is up to you to stay connected and the evidence of doing so will be much fruit.

Fruitfulness is a natural thing. Much of the body of Christ gets this point inverted. Fruit does not produce abiding, but abiding produces fruit. Because the Bible is very clear that fruitfulness is proof of discipleship, and because many Christians would like to be thought of as good disciples, they strive in their own strength to cause something to happen. The ultimate end of this striving is ministry burnout. I have seen evidence that striving is rampant in the fivefold and leadership ranks. They often feel it is their responsibility to cause people to do well, that they are responsible to make churches grow and plant large works. They lose sight of the fact their only responsibility is to stay connected to the source.

I would like to say a little bit about plastic fruit. I see a lot of plastic fruit. It looks good. It's cheap and easy to have a lot of it. It has all the right colors. However, it is very unyielding and isn't very satisfying if you're hungry. There is no moisture in it and it won't quench your thirst. It also lacks the ability to reproduce. There is no seed within it and no plastic apple will ever produce more apples. Sometimes I see churches that are full of plastic fruit. They are loud and robust. They are shiny and colorful. They look really good. They have all sorts of programs that draw more plastic fruit. But there seems to be something missing. Though sometimes the flesh is satisfied, the spirit isn't. Sometimes I think we pastors would like to decorate our churches with plastic fruit rather than the real fruit which takes so much effort. Plastic fruit is easier and takes less time to obtain. It never gets rotten. However, God is only interested in fruit that reproduces fruit. That takes time and abiding, and can never happen unless God causes it to happen. You can plant—you can water—but God causes the increase.

Let's look at the entire passage about abiding verse by verse. This passage is extremely well stated and each verse establishes a point in the step by step of what Jesus is saying.

> *"Abide in Me, and I in you. As the branch cannot bear fruit of itself unless it abides in the vine, so neither can you unless you abide in Me. I am the vine, you are the branches; he who abides in Me and I in him, he bears much fruit, for apart from Me you can do nothing. If anyone does not abide in Me, he is thrown away as a branch and dries up; and they gather them, and cast them into the fire and they are burned. If you abide in Me, and*

My words abide in you, ask whatever you wish, and it will be done for you. My Father is glorified by this, that you bear much fruit, and so prove to be My disciples. Just as the Father has loved Me, I have also loved you; abide in My love. If you keep My commandments, you will abide in My love; just as I have kept My Father's commandments and abide in His love. These things I have spoken to you so that My joy may be in you, and that your joy may be made full."
John 15:4-11

The Logic
"Abide in Me, and I in you. As the branch cannot bear fruit of itself unless it abides in the vine, so neither can you unless you abide in Me."

In the first three sentences of chapter fifteen, Jesus begins to explain His analogy of the relationship of the branches to the vine. This fourth verse is the definition of the cause and effect relationship and explains the goals of this parable. He explains the symbiotic aspects of our relationship to the Lord and our need to maintain this relationship at all costs. This verse defines the logic of what follows. Though this parable does not directly reference the kingdom, since it embodies the goals of kingdom living it is the quintessence of what kingdom living is all about.

The Inevitability
"I am the vine, you are the branches; he who abides in Me and I in him, he bears much fruit, for apart from Me you can do nothing."

Chapter 12

This is absolute cause and effect. For example, if you hold an item above the earth and release it, it will drop to the earth. You don't have to wonder if it will fall to the earth. You don't have to make it fall to the earth. It simply follows the laws of physics and does it. Jesus is saying that fruitfulness has the same relationship to abiding as mass has to gravity.

Jesus is also giving us real insight here about the field dependency of His ambassadors. "Apart from me you can nothing." Let that word, "nothing" settle in a little bit. He is not saying you can do some things but when your goal exceeds your strength, then call on him. He is saying you are helpless apart from Him. It's hard to get very proud about that, isn't it? He also said proof of discipleship is fruit. His Father is glorified by the fact you bear much fruit and so prove to be His disciples. At another time in His ministry, He said "You will know them by their fruit" relating to the distinctive difference between a wolf in sheep's clothing and a true prophet. Just a little aside here. Sitting in a pew every Sunday is not fruit. Doing those things a Christian is expected to do while living their life is not fruit. The words used here are "that which remains." It has substance and visibility. Please also note that this is NOT the fruit of the Spirit. This is a disciple's fruit, not the Holy Spirit's fruit. I believe that a disciple's fruit is discipleship. More disciples and those disciples are ones that remain. Oak trees produce acorns which produce more oak trees. Apples produce apple seeds which produce more apple producing trees. Disciples produce more disciples who produce more disciples and so on. While the evidence of the Holy Spirit being active in you is the production of the fruits the Spirit brings—love, joy, peace, etc., the evidence of you being active in abiding in Christ is fruitfulness in your life as a disciple reproducer. That's kingdom living.

The Antithesis
"If anyone does not abide in Me, he is thrown away as a branch and dries up; and they gather them, and cast them into the fire and they are burned.

The "works" crowd sort of likes this verse. However, Jesus is not presenting an image of God looking down with a critical eye and waiting for the unsuspecting Christian to blow it by not abiding, and then whisking them away to be burned in the fire. It is simply the opposite effect of abiding. The message here is not that you will be burned up if you don't abide, but that you don't need to be burned up because you can abide. I have heard some Christians present Christianity with the harsh message, that you'll go to hell if you don't repent and accept the Lord. Though true enough, it is not the good news we are meant to bring. The approach is not to present the antithesis of our purpose, but to present our purpose in Christ. The message we are to give as ambassadors is, "You don't need to live in death but can have life!" In this instance, Jesus, with the emphasis on the positive outcome of responding correctly, effectively contrasts the result of doing the opposite. This verse is also a cause and effect relationship.

The Promise
"If you abide in Me, and My words abide in you, ask whatever you wish, and it will be done for you."

This promise is real and true. It is as sure as the inevitability of which He spoke in verse five. It is the power of the kingdom—a kingdom where everything done and accomplished is for and by the glory of the Lord. You must eliminate personal agenda for this promise to be relative to you. Way too often people do something for God that is not of God. God doesn't need you to do something for Him but He does want you to do things with Him. Though

He even uses those things you do for Him, you are building with wood, hay, and stubble when you do it in that heart. This sentence is about the living remaining fruit which comes from a vibrant, moment-by-moment walk with God by a Christian who waits continually on Him.

In Isaiah you are told, "They that wait upon the Lord shall renew their strength. They shall rise up on wings as of eagles. They will run and not grow weary. They will walk and not faint." That's what abiding is all about. You are doing all the same things every striving Christian is doing, but you retain your strength and your efforts produce much real fruit. You still run. You still walk. The difference is that you do it with His effort. When you are soaring on this type of power, there is nothing you can't accomplish if the Lord wills it. This is real "giant slaying" power that goes on and on and equips you for exploits far beyond who you would be naturally. There is no burnout associated with this type of power. This is life in the kingdom! It requires abiding and it is the result of abiding.

The Proof
"My Father is glorified by this, that you bear much fruit, and so prove to be My disciples."

Two things are essential to a kingdom walk. One is abiding in Jesus. The other is the established practice of prayer. What is the difference? One is the realization that Christ is your strength and the other is the realization that God is your provider. One of the things I see most commonly in those who seek the kingdom is a tendency to rely on themselves entirely too much. They begin to minister in the power of the Spirit and don't realize when they have run out of supply. When they slowly begin to lose effectiveness, rather than acknowledge their need to replenish, they will try to compensate for their lack of strength by simply exerting more effort. This depletes them further and faster, and as a result their spiritual fruit starts to become rotten. Then, not only do they not have a disciple's fruit but their resident fruit's of the Spirit are rotten as well. I have occasionally found myself at this place. A level of frustration starts to rise and in the midst of that frustration, the thought comes, "Lord, I thought you were with me on this?" His answer is, "I'm with you but you're not with me. Come and spend time in my presence and learn from me. Be still and know that I am God."

It shouldn't be lost on you from this passage that fruit is the evidence of a disciple. One also then may conclude that lack of fruit is proof you are not His disciple. Verse eight has caused many a Christian to stumble in their walk, but only because they want the evidence without the cost. They also often want the glory which belongs to the Father. Because "proof" of a close walk with the Lord is fruit, they go after the fruit rather than the cause of the fruit. Fruit is not the goal. Abiding is the goal, and fruit is the result. You must be brutally honest with yourself about this if you are currently being used by the Lord in some kingdom ministry. Nothing removes a branch from the vine quicker than a desire for recognition of your efforts. You can begin a ministry with all the right motives and suddenly find you are more interested in the kudos than the kingdom. You start your ministry by seeking the Lord and leave it by seeking the glory. Are you growing weary? Are you really tired of the work? Perhaps you've stopped abiding. With abiding, the fruit comes in its season with little effort and you will run and not grow weary—walk and not faint. Stop pursuing fruit, and rather pursue the Lord.

Chapter 12

The Requirement—Obedience

"Just as the Father has loved Me, I have also loved you; abide in My love. If you keep My commandments, you will abide in My love; just as I have kept My Father's commandments and abide in His love."

How important it is to be obedient! Later Jesus tells us His new commandment: that we love one another. He defines that as laying our lives down for each other. Here He simply states the need to obey and the result of obeying. Very often I have found Christians who like being Christians but don't like being around Christians. They like being served by Christians but don't like serving Christians. This is not good. This is contrary to Jesus' commandment and does not lead to abiding. We have been given two arenas for service: The Church, and the world. We are called to serve both. If you are simply attending a church somewhere and not serving within it, then you are not keeping the Lord's commandment. If you serve those in the world and not those in the church you are not keeping this commandment. If you are not keeping His commandments, you are not abiding. If you are not abiding, you are in danger of being burned up—or out. If you want to abide in His love then you must keep His commandments.

Because they often fall in their efforts to obey, many simply quit trying in the areas they have the most difficulty. This produces an effect called "the law of sin and death." Our conscience reminds us when we do wrong, which brings guilt, which produces death in us. Christianity is awesome in how it deals with this effect, however. If you fail—then you confess. You go to the Lord and simply acknowledge your failure as sin, and the blood of Christ cleanses you from the unrighteousness and the death that unrighteousness brings. The Romans 8:2 promise of being set free from the law of sin and death is accomplished. Sin brings death. Death to the soul, to the body, and to the spirit. It is an automatic effect. Confession and repentance brings forgiveness, which brings health and life. As a Christian, you have the advantage of having that effect countered by the cleansing power of the blood of Christ. I John 1:9 says, "If we confess our sins, He is faithful and righteous to forgive us our sins and to cleanse us from all unrighteousness." This is an awesome promise since healthy life is simply a declaration away. You open your mouth, you declare what you just did as wrong, denounce it as sin, and ask for forgiveness. In the next instance, abiding is restored, the effects (not always the reaping) are removed and life is infused into you once again. Because of this provision, when you fail to obey, the effect of obedience can always be restored, because you can soar on the obedience which Jesus accomplished for you.

A non-Christian can repent for their sin all day long, but unless they also accept the Lord, it will never remove from them the guilt and death their sin produces within. It is only when the Spirit which gives life dwells within you, that the blood of Christ can effectively remove the effects guilt brings with it. People pay licensed counselors hundreds of dollars a month to try to have their guilt removed. While counselors attempt to remove the guilt through counseling, they can never accomplish it, since the effect of sin remains. The counselee remains firmly under the law of sin and death. If you're paying a counselor to tell you that what you're doing wrong is okay and that you're okay, save your money. They don't have the ability to help you. Get saved if you're not, confess that what you are doing is sin, and let the blood of Christ cleanse the effects of your sin. If you have already committed your life to Christ, let go of your pride, accept your inability and confess your sin and walk in forgiveness. You are never more than a confession away from abiding—a confession made to your heavenly Father, not an earthly substitute.

Chapter 12

The Purpose
"These things I have spoken to you so that My joy may be in you, and that your joy may be made full."

"That your joy may be made full." Notice that the reason Jesus spoke these things is not to warn you about being cut off and thrown in the fire. Sometimes Christians can be the most negatively focused people on the face of the earth. God is not sitting in heaven with His checklist out, waiting to get us if we blow it. He's waiting for us to move onto His path so He can give us joy. Note that the purpose of Jesus' dissertation is not to produce fruit. That is simply the result. The purpose is so you can have joy and that your joy would not just be minimal, but full. If God is so greatly for you as this then who in the world can successfully be against you?

One can hardly examine the concept of abiding without at least a cursory look at Jesus' instructions on how to pray. Though this chapter is not about the Lord's Prayer, I need to relate to it in reference to prayer in and for the kingdom. It brings to light so much about the purpose of prayer. One time Jesus' disciples came to Him after He got back from praying, and asked Him, "Teach us to pray." Jesus told them to pray in this fashion and spoke the lines often referred to as "The Lord's Prayer." Notice he didn't say, "Pray this prayer." I am not saying that if during your prayer time you quote the lines as a prayer, that you are doing anything wrong. I often use passages of scripture to pray and ask God for something a particular scripture might relate to simply because the scripture says it well and I can know I am praying the Lord's will. I simply want you to be aware that Jesus never spoke those words for the purpose of continual recitation. His intent seems to be to answer the request of his disciples who did not ask, "Give us a prayer to pray," but rather, "teach us to pray."

> *"Pray, then, in this way: 'Our Father who is in heaven, Hallowed be Your name. Your kingdom come. Your will be done, On earth as it is in heaven.'"*
> Matthew 6:9-10

This much-quoted series of instructions tells us His personal emphasis in prayer. The first three lines relate definitively to the kingdom concept. Line one in the transliteration of the Greek is "Hagiostheta to onoma sou." Literally translated this would be "Cause-to-be-made-holy-the-name-yours." When I first saw this verse in the Greek, I wondered why we would need to pray that God would make His name holy. The verb which translates "cause to be made holy" in this sentence is in the imperative voice, which gives it that sense of urgency. Why strongly urge Him to do what one would assume is already the case? Isn't His name already holy? I did not understand this statement until I read this passage from Ezekiel.

> *"It is not for your sake, O house of Israel, that I am about to act, but for My holy name, which you have profaned among the nations where you went. I will vindicate the holiness of My great name which has been profaned among the nations, which you have profaned in their midst. Then the nations will know that I am the LORD," declares the Lord GOD, "when I prove Myself holy among you in their sight."*
> Ezekiel 36:22-23

As you study the Old Testament references to this, you see that the name is profaned by profaning the place where it has been placed. Since the entire family of God has been given that name, we would have to become a holy people for that prayer to be fulfilled. It is interesting to me that the first thing the Lord defines as a needed part of prayer is the urgent request He return us to holiness.

Chapter 12

The Hebrew penchant for triplets is present as Jesus says. "Cause your name to be made holy—cause your kingdom to come and cause your will to be done—and all of it here on earth just as it is in heaven." You see, in heaven, God's kingdom is and was and will continue to be, and in it, His will is always done. It is here we are told to call for His will to be accomplished. Keep in mind, we have been appointed as His ambassadors, so we are the requesting agency for matters taking place in this kingdom of darkness. For this to happen in an effective and world-changing manner, it all must fall under the guidelines of what God wants and wills and how His kingdom should function. In all of that, it is critical that we are maintaining our "set apartness". Holiness is not an avoidance of sin but rather being "set apart unto". As we live our lives surrendered to kingdom principles and standards, we are able to walk in His will and holiness. It is when you surrender your will that you become set apart for God's purposes. You have been put here on earth and brought out of darkness so that you might show forth the works of Him who called you out and gave to you the ministry of reconciliation. You need to be completely set apart.

This prayer has a contemporary application and also a future fulfillment. I believe Jesus was not so much saying to pray for the coming of Him and His kingdom to earth in the ages ahead, but rather to pray that those in His kingdom on earth would respond the same way as those in heaven to His authority and structure. I believe He was telling his disciples to pray that all who were His disciples would function in that same kingdom concept as was to come at another time many, many years later for them, and not so many years hence for us.

The following prayer would fit the instructions Jesus gave His disciples: "Lord help me to be in the world and not of the world so I can be set apart, holy unto You. Make your name holy by making me, who you've placed it on, holy. Let your kingdom come now Lord in my life and my walk with you. Let me walk my life here on this earth doing Your will the same as your servants do in your kingdom in heaven." Such a prayer fits the parameters of the first three lines of instruction Jesus gave his disciples about how they should pray.

The order which Jesus' uses in this set of instructions is not random but defines for us the order of importance. If this is accurate, then His first priority is definitely toward the concept of kingdom, with holiness being primary to that theme.

What is prayer? Many people look at prayer as a shopping list for God. Though you are indeed to bring your needs to the Father, He is not your personal supply clerk. I believe that in order to understand the concept of prayer completely, you must relate to it from the standpoint of your purpose. Since you are appointed as His ambassador and told to bear much fruit, prayer is your source of power and accomplishment. Just as a worldly ambassador can do nothing in his position to benefit the country to which he is assigned apart from his head-of-state, neither can you as a kingdom ambassador accomplish anything in this kingdom without the benefit of working with your head-of-state for the kingdom you are representing. You must stay connected; you must function in your role and you have no authority or power of your own, apart from the impartation from the government you represent. You have certain goals which are central to the kingdom's mission statement and certain goals that are specific to your assignment. To accomplish either requires you maintain your source of supply and your communication to that source. If you do that, you have the promise of the One who has assigned you that you will bear much fruit. You have nothing else required of you but to remain connected and obedient to what He communicates to you, so rest assured, that is where you will find the most resistance as you try to walk as His ambassador.

The most difficult thing about writing this chapter is that the topic of abiding and prayer has such depth. It is hard to simply write one chapter on it, but I will leave this behind, knowing I have only lightly touched on it. I recommend you spend some time asking the same question of the Lord His disciples asked Him: "Lord, teach me to pray."

> *For we do not have a high priest who cannot sympathize with our weaknesses, but One who has been tempted in all things as we are, yet without sin. Therefore let us draw near with confidence to the throne of grace, so that we may receive mercy and find grace to help in time of need.*
> *Hebrews 4:15-16*

Epilogue

"And he carried me away in the Spirit to a great and high mountain, and showed me the holy city, Jerusalem, coming down out of heaven from God, having the glory of God. Her brilliance was like a very costly stone, as a stone of crystal-clear jasper . . . I saw no temple in it, for the Lord God the Almighty and the Lamb are its temple. And the city has no need of the sun or of the moon to shine on it, for the glory of God has illumined it, and its lamp is the Lamb. The nations will walk by its light, and the kings of the earth will bring their glory into it. In the daytime (for there will be no night there) its gates will never be closed; and they will bring the glory and the honor of the nations into it; and nothing unclean, and no one who practices abomination and lying, shall ever come into it, but only those whose names are written in the Lamb's book of life."
Revelation 21:10-11, 22-27

    I wrote this book to give you an understanding of the kingdom of God as it exists on earth today. Let your curiosity drive you to learn more. Study what the word has to say about the kingdom. I urge you to think, question, and seek God.

    Who can walk away from this topic without a sense of awe and wonder at the majesty of His coming kingdom? It will be established in all of its glory, in absolute visibility for a thousand years on this earth! I am not able to end without at least pointing to this great period in future history. This book is not about eschatology, or "end times." That is another book for another time. In my next book, The Millennium, I will address it in great detail. Here I will only reference it lightly.

In the Millennium, we are told Jesus will live with His saints in the city of Jerusalem which will be a place of life, light, and peace. His resurrected saints under His authority will rule and reign the cities of the earth from a new Jerusalem that comes down from heaven. While those thousand years will be an awesome time, for now it is more important to ask the Lord what he would have you do for His kingdom here.

Ask Him—what is His purpose for establishing you now in this age of the kingdom of darkness? Don't live your life as if this carnal life was what mattered most and the next life is just an afterthought. It is here and now He is asking you to serve Him. It is here and now that He has prepared works for you to walk in. Your response here and now establishes your place in the millennial kingdom. It is for a time such as this you were brought into this world to develop a close relationship with Him. Tomorrow will take care of itself, but only on the basis of how you take care of your "today".

Learn to walk, and then learn to run, and then learn to rise high above the kingdom of darkness on the power of the eagle's wings. If you have asked Jesus to be your Lord, you are one of the called of God and a royal priest to the king. Let that truth grip you. Let it excite you. Let the revelation draw you out of this kingdom of darkness and into His marvelous light. Come and be a warrior in the spiritual realms! Stand tall and walk as He would walk. Slay the giants. Ignore the flesh. Enter the kingdom of God!

> "The Spirit and the bride say, "Come." And let the one who hears say, "Come." And let the one who is thirsty come; let the one who wishes take the water of life without cost."
> Revelation 22:17

About The Author
Pastor John Ring

Pastor John came to know the Lord in January of 1975. He received his theological training from Abbot Loop Bible College in Anchorage, Alaska and was ordained in 1989. He was sent out from the church in Anchorage in 1991 and established a Christian counseling center in Hesperia, California, which offered free emotional and family support to non-believers in the community. In 1997, John established a kingdom business which provided Internet access throughout southern California. Three years later, he started a church called "the Place," a Christ-centered church for this generation.

As senior pastor of "the Place," he established relationships with several other churches in southern California. He and his church also partner with a number of African churches in Cote d'Ivoire, Kenya, Lesotho, and Ghana. He and his wife are happily married and have four children. Pastor John is currently writing a book called The Millennium which is scheduled for release in 2008.

A TALE OF
TWO KINGDOMS

Orders for additional copies or bulk distribution can be
made by visiting
www.attheplace.org/2kingdoms
or by sending a written request to
The Place in the Desert (DBA "the Place")
13550 Sky Court,
Victorville, California, 92392, U.S.A.